Understanding

Flowers for Algernon

New and future titles in the Understanding Great Literature
series include:

Understanding *The Catcher in the Rye*
Understanding *Hamlet*
Understanding *I Am the Cheese*
Understanding *The Outsiders*
Understanding *Romeo and Juliet*
Understanding *The Yearling*

Understanding

Flowers for Algernon

UNDERSTANDING GREAT LITERATURE

Patrice Cassedy

Lucent Books
P.O. Box 289011
San Diego, CA 92198-9011

On Cover: Daniel Keyes, author of *Flowers for Algernon.*

Quotations from *Algernon, Charlie, and I* by Daniel Keyes are reprinted by permission of the author; © 1959, 1966, 1999 by Daniel Keyes.

Quotations from *Flowers for Algernon* by Daniel Keyes are reprinted by permission of Harcourt, Inc.; © 1966 and renewed 1994 by Daniel Keyes

Library of Congress Cataloging-in-Publication Data

Cassedy, Patrice.
    Understanding Flowers for Algernon / by Patrice Cassedy.
        p. cm.—(Understanding great literature)
    Includes bibliographical references and index.
    Summary: Discusses the young adult book "Flowers for Algernon" by Daniel Keyes, including the author's life, the science fiction genre, and the book's plot, characters, and themes.
    ISBN 1-56006-784-5 (alk. paper)
    1. Keyes, Daniel. Flowers for Algernon. 2. Mentally handicapped in literature. [1. Keyes, Daniel. Flowers for Algernon. 2. American Literature—History and criticism.] I. Title. II. Series.
    PS3561.E769 F583 2001
    813'.54—dc21

00-009157

Copyright 2001 by Lucent Books, Inc.
P.O. Box 289011, San Diego, California 92198-9011

Printed in the U.S.A.

Contents

FOREWORD

"Except for a living man, there is nothing more wonderful than a book!" wrote the widely respected nineteenth-century teacher and writer Charles Kingsley. A book, he continued, "is a message to us from human souls we never saw. And yet these [books] arouse us, terrify us, teach us, comfort us, open our hearts to us as brothers." There are many different kinds of books, of course; and Kingsley was referring mainly to those containing literature—novels, plays, short stories, poems, and so on. In particular, he had in mind those works of literature that were and remain widely popular with readers of all ages and from many walks of life.

Such popularity might be based on one or several factors. On the one hand, a book might be read and studied by people in generation after generation because it is a literary classic, with characters and themes of universal relevance and appeal. Homer's epic poems, the *Iliad* and the *Odyssey,* Chaucer's *Canterbury Tales,* Shakespeare's *Hamlet* and *Romeo and Juliet,* and Dickens's *A Christmas Carol* fall into this category. Some popular books, on the other hand, are more controversial. Mark Twain's *Huckleberry Finn* and J. D. Salinger's *The Catcher in the Rye,* for instance, have their legions of devoted fans who see them as great literature; while others view them as less than worthy because of their racial depictions, profanity, or other factors.

Still another category of popular literature includes realistic modern fiction, including novels such as Robert Cormier's *I Am the Cheese* and S. E. Hinton's *The Outsiders.* Their keen social insights and sharp character portrayals have consistently reached out to and captured the imaginations of many teenagers and young adults; and for this reason they are often assigned and studied in schools.

These and other similar works have become the "old standards" of the literary scene. They are the ones that people most often read, discuss, and study; and each has, by virtue of its content, critical success, or just plain longevity, earned the right to be the subject of a book examining its content. (Some, of course, like the *Iliad* and *Hamlet,* have been the subjects of numerous books already; but their literary stature is so lofty that there can never be too many books about them!) For millions of readers and students in one generation after another, each of these works becomes, in a sense, an adventure in appreciation, enjoyment, and learning.

The main purpose of Lucent's Understanding Great Literature series is to aid the reader in that ongoing literary adventure. Each volume in the series focuses on a single literary work that a majority of critics and teachers view as a classic and/or that is widely studied and discussed in schools. A typical volume first tells why the work in question is important. Then follow detailed overviews of the author's life, the work's historical background, its plot, its characters, and its themes. Numerous quotes from the work, as well as by critics and other experts, are interspersed throughout and carefully documented with footnotes for those who wish to pursue further research. Also included is a list of ideas for essays and other student projects relating to the work, an appendix of literary criticisms and analyses by noted scholars, and a comprehensive annotated bibliography.

The great nineteenth-century American poet Henry David Thoreau once quipped: "Read the best books first, or you may not have a chance to read them at all." For those who are reading or about to read the "best books" in the literary canon, the comprehensive, thorough, and thoughtful volumes of the Understanding Great Literature series are indispensable guides and sources of enrichment.

A Man of His Time

Daniel Keyes's science fiction novel, *Flowers for Algernon*, was published in 1966, seven years after the original version—a short story by the same name—appeared in the *Magazine of Fantasy and Science Fiction*. The short story and novel both received top awards from science fiction associations. The novel has sold millions of copies around the world and has never gone out of print. It was recently included in a series of modern classic books. The popular 1968 movie *Charly* was based on the book, as were two television movies, the most recent of which aired in 2000.

The enduring popularity of Keyes's story can, in part, be attributed to the author's use of first-person narration, which allows the reader to truly understand the feelings and desires of its main character, Charlie Gordon. But the novel's lasting appeal stems from the issues and themes it presents. For although *Flowers for Algernon* is a science fiction tale, it expresses human desires, shortcomings, and weaknesses that are ageless and strike a common chord in most readers.

A Compelling Plot

Keyes presents his themes through a diary (a collection of "progress reports") written by Charlie, a mentally challenged man who becomes brilliant through experimental brain surgery. Although scientists in the twenty-first century are striving for ways to improve human beings, when *Flowers for Algernon* was written, the notion that scientists could increase intelligence was purely imaginary. This fantasy aspect is the reason the novel is considered science fiction. But while many science fiction authors dwell on scientific or technical details, Keyes concentrated instead on developing a very real-seeming character whose experiences cause the reader to consider the book's important issues and themes.

The reader's appreciation of Charlie's situation begins on the first page of the novel when Charlie writes that he wants to be smart. In Charlie's childlike view, being smart means talking about important things like politics with the guys at work or being promoted to a more challenging position. Most important of all, to Charlie, being smart means being loved.

Charlie's dream of intelligence comes true. Scientists make him smart, using the same kind of brain operation that worked on a mouse named Algernon. Within weeks, Charlie is more brilliant than the scientists. He can talk about philosophy. He learns languages. He masters mathematics.

But Charlie cannot find love. Suddenly, he is too brilliant to get along with his coworkers, who do not understand the change in him. He becomes arrogant and alienates even the scientists who helped him. When he visits his mother, she does not appreciate that he is a changed man. She rejects him, just as she did when he was a child. His visit to his father is unsatisfying too. Charlie poses as a customer in his father's barbershop. Although his father gives Charlie a haircut and shave, he never recognizes his son. Worst of all, Charlie cannot build a meaningful romantic relationship with Alice, the adult-school teacher who originally recommended him for the surgery and helps him become brilliant.

Besides the inability to connect with others, there is a more pressing tragedy in store for Charlie: he discovers, through the death of Algernon, that the experiment is destined to fail. Soon

In a scene from the 1968 film Charly *doctors introduce Charly to Algernon, a mouse who has just undergone the same intelligence-enhancing brain surgery proposed for Charly (spelled Charlie in the book).*

after Algernon dies, Charlie gradually slips back into mental retardation. He retains enough emotional awareness to realize that other people pity him, including Alice, who cries when she sees him returning to his former self. In the end, instead of facing the humiliation of his old life, Charlie commits himself to isolation, hiding away in a home for the mentally challenged, far from the people and life he knew.

A Human Tragedy

The story's sad ending caused problems for Daniel Keyes. Several publishers refused to publish the book because it was not uplifting. The publishers believed that readers would prefer to see Charlie remain smart so he and Alice could marry. Keyes refused. For him, the power of the book came from the fact that Charlie tragically loses his brilliance. Only through this plot device could Keyes express his themes and make readers wonder whether the desire to reach beyond one's capabilities is a dangerous wish and whether science should be used to effect such "improvements."

Readers and movie viewers wholeheartedly agreed with Keyes's decision to write the book as a tragedy. They developed a genuine sympathy for Charlie's situation. His loneliness, his need for love, his wish that he could have both intelligence and affection resonate with those who meet Charlie through Keyes's story. Nearly fifty years after Charlie Gordon was created, he still finds his way into the hearts of readers and movie viewers around the world.

CHAPTER ONE

A Biography of Daniel Keyes

N ovelists do not always begin their working lives as novelists, and Daniel Keyes was no exception. Keyes sailed with the U.S. Maritime Service, edited short stories for pulp magazines, scripted comics, co-owned a photography studio, and taught high school and college before publishing *Flowers for Algernon*, his first novel, in 1966.

Daniel Keyes, who was born August 9, 1927, in Brooklyn, New York, chose a career that suited his talents. But authoring books was not the future Betty and William Keyes had in mind for their oldest child. They believed he should become a doctor, perhaps because their own career options were limited by their status as immigrants. Both Betty and William were born in Europe and lived in Canada before immigrating to the United States, where they met in New York City. Neither had much formal schooling, although William had learned English, French, and Russian as a boy while working for trappers in Quebec. In contrast to the life they imagined for their son, Betty and William maintained a modest household in New York, with Betty working as a beautician and William, who was sometimes out of work, taking on various jobs.

An Early Love of Books

Having resolved that her son would become a doctor, Betty set her mind to guiding him toward that end. She monitored his homework throughout his early school years. She was a strict taskmaster, tearing out pages of his composition notebooks she deemed unsatisfactory and waking him early to study for math tests. Although these efforts enhanced Keyes's skills as a student, what created the most lasting impression were the many hours Betty spent reading to him. From this bedtime ritual, Keyes grew to love stories, so much so that he later remarked that he "always wanted to become a writer."[1]

Keyes's earliest experience as a storyteller is related in his autobiography, *Algernon, Charlie and I: A Writer's Journey.* While working at the beauty parlor, Betty asked Daniel to entertain the unruly daughter of a customer. The only way Keyes could keep the girl's attention was by bringing out an armload of books and pretending to read, an event he describes in the present tense in his autobiography:

> Though the girl keeps crying, I don't stop. Eventually, she grows silent and listens. Of course, I can't really read at that age, but my mother has read the stories to me so often that I know them by heart.
>
> "He can read!" one of the customers says.
> The girl's mother asks, "How old is he?"
> "Three and a half," my mother says proudly.
> "He must be a genius."
> She opens her purse and takes out a penny.
> "That was very clever, Danny. Here, buy a piece of candy."[2]

After this success, Keyes was hooked on storytelling, and he continued to look for opportunities to show off his talent. One evening when he was six or seven he watched a boy named Sammy recite a story to a group of kids outside the grocery store. The young audience was so intent on Sammy's story that when he stopped and said he would continue another time, they yelled with disappointment. But no matter how angry the kids became about Sammy's techniques, they always returned to hear the next installment of the story. Keyes longed to tell stories just like Sammy, but because he was far younger than the other boys, he was at first afraid to join in. To get up his nerve, he practiced at home, inventing tales at night in bed. He eventually became a popular storyteller, winning the approval of neighborhood kids with the exciting plots he made up and recited. More than ever, Daniel was hooked on stories. He longed to become a writer, but, as he explains in his autobiography, he was not ready to defy his parents' wishes:

> Ever since I was a child, [my parents] had decided I would become a doctor. When I asked why, my father answered, "Because a doctor is like God. He cures people and saves lives."
>
> My mother added, "When you were a baby, you had an infected mastoid and double pneumonia. A wonderful doctor saved your life."
>
> My father said, "We want you to cure people and save lives."
>
> I accepted their reasons and their obligation. I would work hard, take part-time jobs to earn money and go to college and medical school. I would become a doctor. Since I loved my parents, I buried my dream of becoming a writer. . . . Secretly, I wondered if I could become both doctor and writer.[3]

As Keyes understood from a young age, doing well in school was only one part of fulfilling his parents' dream that he attend college and medical school. In addition, he would need money to pay tuition and living expenses. Beginning when he was eight or nine years old, Keyes came up with resourceful ways to earn money. He sold lunches from a little red wagon to women working at a garment factory, delivered tuxedos, made screwdrivers, and served frozen custard. Beginning at age fourteen, he delivered bagels on the way to junior high school. The schedule was grueling, requiring him to get up at three in the morning to begin work. When he had finished, the driver would drop him off to start his school day. During high school at Thomas Jefferson High School in Brooklyn, Keyes worked in a luncheonette.

In the Merchant Marine

Although Keyes was complying with his parents' dictum to work hard at school, he was a voracious reader and much preferred the imaginary world of books to the real world of school. In time, he found that a wedge was growing between him and his parents. As he explains in his autobiography, beginning in adolescence, "I discovered the more I read and learned, the less I could communicate with them. I was losing them—drifting away into my world of books and stories."[4]

Keyes's intellectual alienation from his parents increased during his freshman year as a pre-med major at New York University. By the end of that year, at the age of seventeen, he was feeling more restless than ever. He had spent all the money he had saved for college, and his motivation to become a doctor was at an all-time low. He needed to get away. It was 1945 and with World War II still raging, many of his friends were enlisting in the armed forces. Keyes's first choice was to join the navy, but because his poor eyesight disqualified him, Keyes chose another path, which he describes in his autobiography: "I knew that joining the U.S. Maritime Service [merchant marine] would be a turning point. I would be away from my parents, living my own life, pursuing my own dreams."[5]

Because he was not yet eighteen, Keyes needed his parents' permission to join the service. They reluctantly agreed, but only after he promised to complete his medical education upon his return. Finally free to start his adventure, Keyes became a merchant marine purser, an administrative post that included running the onboard store and doling out sailors' pay. Because no one else was available, he was also assigned to act as a pharmacist's mate, tending to sailors' medical problems, which, for the most part, were minor. "That left me lots of time to read and write. I used my office typewriter to try my hand at writing sketches from my past and keeping my personal journal for material to store away for the sea novel I knew I would write someday."[6]

Keyes also took advantage of the ship's library to develop his writing skills, using the learning method of the famous author, Somerset Maugham, who had copied passages in longhand from his favorite writers. As Keyes explains in his autobiography, "I believed that, like Maugham, I would eventually outgrow imitation, but by then I would have learned to shape words into sentences, and to mold them into paragraphs. I trusted myself to develop an ear for language, and to find my own voice and personal style, as well as those of my characters. Since Maugham hadn't been too proud to learn to write as children do—by imitation—neither was I."[7]

Daniel Keyes developed his writing skills using techniques employed by famous author Somerset Maugham (pictured).

While Keyes used his time in the merchant marine to foster his dream of becoming a writer, he also had an experience that led to a final career decision. As a pharmacist's mate, he was once called upon to treat a sailor who had binged on bad alcohol. In spite of Keyes's valiant efforts to revive the unconscious man, the patient died. From that incident, Keyes knew for certain what he always suspected: he was a writer by nature, not a doctor.

An Education in Psychology

Keyes left the merchant marine at the age of nineteen. After informing his parents that he had chosen to become a writer, he moved into a small apartment in New York City. There he wrote the novel about a teenaged ship's purser, a work he had envisioned while he was in the service. When he failed to find a publisher who was interested, he realized he would have to earn money another way while honing his writing skills. He enrolled at Brooklyn College as a psychology major, believing that the life of a lay psychoanalyst (a therapist without a medical degree) would provide a decent income, but "might leave me energy and time to write."[8]

Keyes describes the other benefits he saw for a novelist working as a therapist: "I would learn about peoples' motives, and come to understand their conflicts. And I imagined how that would help me create believable characters—living, suffering, changing characters—for my stories and novels."[9] Keyes graduated with a bachelor of arts degree in psychology in 1950. He then took one year of postgraduate work at the City College of New York (CCNY), where he also studied psychology. During that time he worked selling advertising. Through this position he met a friend who invited him to hang out at a photography studio in New York City. There, Keyes met a fashion stylist named Aurea Vazquez. Keyes returned often on his way to class at CCNY to visit Aurea, and the two grew closer.

Breaking into Print

Although Keyes never did become a psychoanalyst, his studies of the human mind allowed him to skillfully portray Charlie and the other real characters that appear in his writings. His chosen career path finally opened up to him in his early twenties when he got a job offer in publishing. In his autobiography, *Algernon, Charlie and I: A Writer's Journey,* Keyes explained how a friend's literary agent arranged an interview for the job by stretching the truth about Keyes's publishing experience:

> One Friday afternoon [in September 1950], I got a call from a writer-acquaintance named Lester del Rey. He wanted to know if I was interested in a job as associate fiction editor for [Stadium Publishing, which sold] a chain of pulps. These were the popular fiction magazines of the day, printed on cheap, untrimmed stock that left paper dandruff all over your dark clothing. . . . [Del Rey's agent wrote a note that] said I'd worked at his literary agency for about six months on a temporary job, and had experience doing pulp reading for another periodical.[10]

Although Keyes was a bit nervous about presenting himself as having experience he did not have, he interviewed well. After a two-week trial at Stadium, during which he refrained from seeing Aurea because he had so much to learn, Keyes was officially given the title of associate fiction editor. He immersed himself in selecting short stories for the publisher's western, sports, and science fiction magazines from work submitted by agents and writers. Not long after he started with Stadium, a fortunate twist of fate led to the publication of Keyes's first short story under an assumed name. The story was a western and, as Keyes later reflected, it was no masterpiece.

Keyes's lucky break came when an advertiser withdrew a large ad from one of the Stadium western magazines at the last minute. As an editor, Keyes was responsible for making sure that any pages that did not contain advertising included stories or novelettes. When the advertiser withdrew the ad just before the issue was ready to print, Keyes was told to replace it with a three-thousand-word story. But he did not have an appropriate story of that length in his files. Instead, he wrote one himself. Using an assumed name, he submitted the story to the magazine through an agent, then convinced his boss, who was not too impressed, that he should give the "new" writer a chance. Over time, other stories by Daniel Keyes found their way into Stadium magazines through anonymous channels. As their number grew, the quality of the stories improved significantly.

First Short Stories

By the time an editor asked Keyes to submit a story for a 1952 issue of *Other Worlds Science Stories*, the author knew what he was doing. He wrote "Robot Unwanted," which was chosen as the lead story for the issue. Keyes was elated, as he writes in his autobiography:

> [The story was] 5,000 words long, and the check, after a 10% deduction for the agent's fee, was for $90.00. The one copy I still have, is on crumbling pulp paper, and as I open to it the page comes loose. The blurb reads: *"Robert was the only one on Earth—an F.R. That meant he was a free robot; free to do anything he wanted—but he didn't want to die!"*[11]

Keyes kept writing science fiction stories, publishing two more in 1952 and a third in 1958. During that period he lost his job at Stadium Publishing because American readers had come to prefer paperback novels, and the pulp magazines were going out of business. In a recent interview, Keyes described his next career move: "So I moved to Timely Comics [where] I wrote tons and tons of fantasy comics, horror comics, and I earned a good living that way. That was my ghostwriting period."[12]

The ghostwriting period was an important one for Keyes. He gained extensive experience creating stories, and began to consider seriously the story idea that developed into *"Flowers for Algernon."* As he puts it, "[T]he idea behind 'Flowers' was originally intended as a comics fantasy/science fiction story. 'What would happen if it were possible to increase human intelligence?'"[13]

His relationship with Aurea also flourished. They were married in 1952 and lived in his inexpensive apartment in New York City. Keyes continued to write, but still needed another income to support himself and his new wife. They invested in the photography studio where Aurea had worked. When that business failed, Keyes turned to teaching English and creative writing, starting in 1954 at Thomas Jefferson High School in Brooklyn, which he had attended as a boy. He taught one year, left, then returned to teach again from 1957 to 1962.

Finding Charlie

Keyes never forgot his idea for a story about a man whose intelligence is increased, but he could not figure out how to get started on it. When he went back to teaching high school the second time, he was assigned a special education class. There he finally had an experience that allowed him to imagine who his man of increased intelligence might be. He described this important event in a 1997 interview:

> I had about 50 false starts, in searching for the character who has his intelligence increased. Who would be Charlie Gordon? I had a plumber, a truck driver, a criminal—a few pages, and it didn't go anywhere. I put it aside. . . . [My] very first week of teaching a class of slow learners, a boy sitting in the back came up to me and said, "Mr. Keyes, this is a dummy class, isn't it? If I try hard and I get smart before the end of the term, would you put me into a regular class? I want to be smart."[14]

From this impression, Charlie Gordon came to life. Keyes quickly wrote the short story, "Flowers for Algernon," submitting it, at the publisher's request, to *Galaxy*, the magazine that had published Keyes's third story. To Keyes's surprise, the editor insisted that he change the ending to a happy one in which Charlie would stay smart and marry Alice. But Keyes had in mind to write a tragedy. He stuck to his goal and sold the story instead to the *Magazine of Fantasy and Science Fiction*. Released in 1959, "Flowers for Algernon" immediately became a classic among science fiction fans, winning a Hugo, the major award of the World Science Fiction Society. The first television adaptation appeared in 1961. During that year, Keyes also accomplished his goal of earning a higher degree that would allow him to teach at the college level, a master's degree in English and American literature from Brooklyn College.

The Root Cellar of the Mind

Keyes continued to write short stories and published five more between 1960 and 1992, including one called "Spellbinder" that told the story of Sammy, the boy who inspired Keyes to become a neighborhood storyteller. But after publishing "Flowers for Algernon" in the late 1950s, Keyes was haunted by a sense that there was more to Charlie than he had included in the short story. He wanted to tell about the character's childhood, and to do that he knew he needed to write a novel. With a master's degree, he was qualified to work as a college instructor. He accepted a position teaching English literature at Wayne State University in Detroit, Michigan. There he began to hammer out the details of the novel.

Once again, his education in psychology proved useful, this time to assist him in the writing process. Keyes had undergone psychotherapy during his college studies, a requirement for everyone training to become a psychoanalyst. Lying on an analyst's couch, allowing his thoughts to wander in the Freudian technique known as free association, taught Keyes how his character Charlie might behave or be treated in a similar situation. But it also provided Keyes with an important creative tool, as he writes in his autobiography. "I use free-association like a gardener's spade to dig out connected memories, bring them into the light and replant them where they can bloom."[15]

Keyes sees the process of remembering events from his past as discovering what has been stored in the "root cellar" of his mind. The root cellar metaphor itself originated in a childhood memory. When Keyes was small, he discovered a place in the basement where his parents stored his old toys. "Somewhere between the coalbin and the furnace—in the root cellar of my mind—ideas, images, scenes and dreams wait in the dark until I need them."[16]

In his autobiography, Keyes highlights events from his early years that stocked the root cellar of his mind for later use in the novel *Flowers for Algernon*. One interesting memory is of his father's junk shop, which Keyes visited around the age of eight. He was fascinated by a huge pile of discarded books that his father and another man were preparing for recycling into paper. Knowing how much his son loved books, William Keyes said Daniel could choose some books to take home. Climbing up the pile of books and deciding which to save was an experience Keyes never forgot.

> The image of myself as a boy going up and then coming down Book Mountain is fixed in my memory as the icon of my love of reading and learning. It was clear to me as I wrote [the short story] "Flowers for Algernon" where the shape of it came from. As Charlie's intelligence increases, I visualize him ascending a mountain. The higher he climbs, the farther he sees, until at the peak, he turns and sees all around him the world of knowledge—of good and evil. But then he must come down the other side.[17]

Another important event that Keyes stored in his mental root cellar occurred when he was a teenager working at the luncheonette. While waiting on tables one evening, he had an unfortunate mishap that helped him understand how Charlie might feel in a similar situation; Keyes dropped a tray of coffee creamers and sandwich plates, causing the diners to laugh and applaud. Since he was waiting on important customers, his boss became furious and yelled that Keyes was a moron. Fed up, Keyes quit the job. But he never forgot the experience and used it to write the scene where Charlie sees a mentally handicapped busboy drop a tray of glasses. "I was able to see it through Charlie's eyes and feel his emotions. I was able to write it, because it happened to me."[18]

A Race to Publish

Keyes knew that if he did not sell the novel before his lectureship at Wayne State ended in 1966, he would not be able to continue teaching at the college level without earning yet another degree, a doctor of philosophy. He worked hard to finish the novel, and sent it to a publisher who had given him a $650 advance. But the publisher found some of the book disturbing and believed it should contain more proven plot elements, such as a love triangle or a dramatic confrontation between Charlie and the scientists.

Keyes did not change the book to include these plot elements, but he did make substantial revisions that he thought improved the novel. He submitted the revision to the same publisher, but without success: early in 1964, he received word that the publisher would not buy the book. Keyes rode out his despair at being rejected, and submitted the book to other publishers, who also rejected the book. Just as his lectureship at Wayne State was about to end, he made the important sale to a publisher then known as Harcourt, Brace and World. The book was a tremendous success, receiving a

Nebula Award, the highest award given by the Science Fiction and Fantasy Writers of America.

While Keyes had been working on the novel, actor Cliff Robertson had been consulting with Keyes and working on a movie based on the short story. The 1968 movie *Charly* was a major hit, and Robertson won an Academy Award for his portrayal of Charly Gordon.

Later Publications

When the lectureship in Detroit ended, Keyes, his wife Aurea, and their two young daughters, Hillary Ann and Leslie Joan, moved to Athens, Ohio. There, Keyes made a career at Ohio University, first as a lecturer, then as a professor of English and director of the creative writing center. He continued writing, publishing *The Touch* in 1968. Set in a fictional city outside Detroit, the novel is another example of Keyes's interest in the impact of scientific advances on human beings. In this story, society ostracizes a young couple because they have been exposed to radiation through an accident at the husband's work.

Keyes's third novel, *The Fifth Sally*, published in 1980, tells the story of Sally Porter, a "drab waitress, divorcee, and loner" who has four other personalities, including a vicious one called Jinx. The novel is "the first contemporary novel to deal with the theme [of multiple personality disorder] as fiction."[19]

The Fifth Sally illustrates Keyes's continuing fascination with "the complexities of the human mind."[20] Building on his interest in multiple personality disorders, Keyes undertook the challenging task of writing a true-crime story about a man with twenty-four distinct personalities. *The Minds of Billy Milligan* was published in 1981. Billy Milligan was arrested for kidnapping and raping three women, but was acquitted "of his crimes by reason of insanity caused by multiple personality—the first such decision in history."[21]

Keyes undertook the project only after he had received the consent of Billy Milligan himself. In order to obtain this consent,

Keyes sent Milligan a copy of *Flowers for Algernon.* "It was only after several of Milligan's selves read *Flowers for Algernon* that they agreed among themselves to work with the author."[22]

The Minds of Billy Milligan won a special award from the Mystery Writers of America. Keyes's next book, *Unveiling Claudia: A True Story of a Serial Murder*, was a nonfiction account of a crime involving schizophrenia. This work earned Keyes an Edgar nomination from the Mystery Writers of America. A second book on the topic, *The Milligan Wars*—a book about

The novels of author Daniel Keyes explore the fascinating complexities of the human mind.

multiple personality disorders—was published in Japan in 1994. An American release is expected at the time a pending movie version is released.

An Autobiography

After years of grappling with difficult psychological themes, Keyes decided to tell the world how he came to write his most popular book, *Flowers for Algernon.* His autobiography, *Algernon, Charlie and I: A Writer's Journey*, was released in 1999. In this book, the author explains the life events that inspired him to write his most famous book. He also gives the reader insight into the process of writing and selling a novel, and explains what happens when a book is adapted to film.

Although the 1968 movie *Charly* was received extremely well by the public, there were scenes that Keyes felt were not true to the novel's characterization of Charlie. For Keyes, Charlie is a man who, although confused and arrogant at the height of his brilliance, never loses a basically decent nature. Therefore, Keyes argues in the autobiography that the movie scenes of Charlie's forcing himself on Alice and joining a drug cult were untrue to the original characterization. Most bothersome to Keyes, according to the autobiography, is the movie's lack of focus on "the agony of the downward curve of Charlie's deterioration."[23] This is the part of the story that Keyes fought to preserve in spite of the objections of publishers. They believed it too painful for science fiction fans, who were used to lighter fare.

In addition to taking on a life of its own in the medium of film, a novel impacts readers' lives, often in ways an author does not anticipate. Connecting with readers is why Keyes writes, a fact that he best understood after students who read the novel for class wrote to Keyes to say that *Flowers for Algernon* helped them better understand their problems and those of others. In Keyes's words, "I write in the hope that, long after I'm gone, my stories and books, like pebbles dropped into water, will continue to spread in widening circles and touch other minds."[24]

The Future

Good fiction affects readers in meaningful ways, but *science* fiction may actually go beyond its pages to become reality. For Keyes, this possibility has occurred in his lifetime. In an afterword to his autobiography, he describes a newspaper article he read in the *New York Times* in the fall of 1999. The article reported that scientists had created a smarter mouse using genetic engineering techniques that could some day be used to improve human memory. Keyes was astonished, because science appeared to be catching up with science fiction far sooner than he had imagined. Algernon, the mouse of his story, finally had a real-life counterpart. As Keyes describes it, he contacted the lead researcher in the project, Dr. Joe Z. Tsien at Princeton University, and asked if it will someday be possible to increase human intelligence. Keyes was astonished to learn that Tsien believes it will be possible in the next thirty years.

Although Keyes's other books have received mostly positive reviews, only *The Minds of Billy Milligan* is currently in print in the United States. However, *Flowers for Algernon* has been in print continuously since its publication and has been sold in dozens of countries in many different languages. It has inspired television, movie, and stage adaptations around the world. As an indication of its importance in twentieth-century literature, *Flowers for Algernon* was released in 1995 as part of the Harcourt Brace Modern Classic series. The most recent television movie version aired in February 2000. Keyes's other books enjoy great popularity outside of the states—for example, *The Fifth Sally* is a best-seller in Japan.

Keyes is highly selective when deciding on a new project and, in a 1997 interview, explained that he works only with themes and plots that he considers important and original. If these criteria are met, he applies an additional test before beginning the project. "I put [the story] away and try *not* to write it. If it demands to be written, and comes up in my dreams and my thoughts periodically when I'm not paying attention, then I get the message, and I will commit myself to work on it."[25] That commitment is still very much part of Keyes's life, and, at age seventy-two, he continues to write every day.

CHAPTER TWO

Science Fiction in a Time of Change

Flowers for Algernon is a work of science fiction. Science fiction is a relatively new form of fiction that, as scholars have written, "can be most broadly defined as a literary response to the rise of modern science."[26] Science has always attempted to expand human knowledge, and science fiction has often used the quest for knowledge as a key theme. Flowers for Algernon is a work that follows this theme, but instead of visualizing the potential rewards of the quest, Keyes's novel considers the possible tragic costs. Keyes's work is not the first to ponder the negative consequences of scientific advances. In fact, according to one writer, in science fiction the thirst for knowledge is "often shown as ambiguous, unsettling, even paradoxical."[27] As a novel written from this perspective, Flowers for Algernon joins other works of science fiction that question whether the benefits of greater knowledge are worth the price paid for them.

Science Fiction Supermen

Because of its subject matter, Flowers for Algernon can be classified as intelligence or superman science fiction. This type of science fiction deals with characters that are abnormally intelligent.

The first example of such a work is *The Hampdenshire Wonder*, by J. D. Beresford. Written in 1911, it draws a conclusion similar to that of *Flowers for Algernon*, namely that super intelligence does not necessarily bring about well-being. Born a supergenius, the child in *The Hampdenshire Wonder* becomes so brilliant that he develops contempt for books, which, he believes, express a human wisdom that is beneath his newfound intellect. He soon finds that he can no longer communicate with anyone. His father abandons him. Devastated and lonely, he commits suicide at the age of seven.

Other superman fiction followed. The man born a supergenius in Olaf Stapledon's *Odd John*, published in 1935, also despairs and finally commits suicide. His story is similar to Charlie's in that he educates himself with amazing speed and finds he is intellectually above other humans. But he is different from Charlie in one important way. Charlie is emotionally immature, yet remains moral. As critic John J. Pierce explains, Stapledon's hero "comes to see himself as beyond the norms of human morality as well as beyond human intelligence—incest, robbery, even murder are justified in the name of his survival and awakening."[28]

The hero of Stanley G. Weinbaum's 1939 novel *The New Adam* also commits suicide because, according to critic John J. Pierce, the man finds that brilliance does not bring him happiness. To illustrate this point, Pierce quotes from the novel: "With the growth of intellect, happiness becomes an elusive quantity, so that doubtless the Superman, when he arrives, will be of all creatures the most unhappy."[29]

America After World War II

Although *Flowers for Algernon* is part of a legacy of science fiction dealing with increasing intellect, the tale is also a product of its times. Keyes published the short story "Flowers for Algernon" in 1959 and the novel in 1966, in an era when Americans were experiencing the power of science to dramatically improve the quality of life. Medical advances were occurring at an astonishing rate, changing lives in dramatic ways. Jonas Salk developed a polio vaccine. A kidney was successfully transplanted from one human to another. Procedures to implant artificial heart valves were developed. Science was capable of prolonging life, and many scientists were seen as miracle workers.

In 1953, researchers James Watson and Francis Crick, building on recent work of colleagues, created a model of the double-helix structure of DNA. This accomplishment led to rapid advances in the field of biotechnology, specifically in the field of genetic engineering, which science writer Francis Leone suggests "holds more promise for the future and peoples' well-being"[30] than any other field of genetics. Discoveries that followed from the modeling of DNA led to the identification and treatment of genetic diseases as well as the production of such beneficial substances as insulin and human growth hormone.

But at the time *Flowers for Algernon* was conceived, the United States was also experiencing the frightening power of scientific advances. Less than fifteen years before Keyes published the short story version of the novel, American atomic bombs exploded in the Japanese cities of Hiroshima and Nagasaki, killing more than two hundred thousand people. Scientists working in the United States had created the nuclear threat, but in 1962 that threat was turned on Americans in a location closer to home than ever before. That year the U.S. military discovered that Soviet ships had placed missiles on Cuba, off the coast of Florida, well within range of Washington, D.C., and American strategic military bases. Historian Martin Walker describes the episode like this: "The next thirteen days were the most dangerous period of the Cold War [the rivalry for world influence between the Americans and the Soviet Communists]. A nuclear exchange was so close that both White House and [Soviet] Kremlin officials frankly expected the bombs to fall."[31] While the Soviets finally backed down, few Americans alive in 1962 have forgotten their fear that they were about to die in a nuclear war.

In the field of medicine, the race to improve the quality of life was also exhibiting a dark side. In 1961, the drug thalidomide, released in Europe to treat nausea in pregnant women, was found to cause catastrophic birth defects. Thousands of babies were born malformed.

While *Flowers for Algernon* does not incorporate these world events specifically, the novel can be seen as a cautionary tale that reflects society's ambivalence about the benefits of modern science. Keyes's attitude can be seen most obviously in the structure of the novel. Instead of writing about a scientific experiment that succeeded and brought happiness to its subject, Keyes penned a tragedy that shows the dark side of science, a subject on the minds of Americans of his generation.

Psychological Advances

Just as twentieth-century scientific advances altered the treatment of physical illnesses and conditions, advances in the field of psychology changed the way psychological problems and conditions were treated. Two significant psychological developments figure prominently in *Flowers for Algernon*. One is the widespread acceptance of psychological classification methods that include intelligence and personality tests. The other is a method of therapy called psychoanalysis, commonly used to treat psychological problems.

The psychological events of the twentieth century are portrayed skillfully by Keyes, who studied psychology in college and in graduate school. In the novel, Charlie is frequently referred to as a "moron," a term that was medically accepted when *Flowers for Algernon* was written. Use of the term by the medical community began in 1910 at a meeting of the American Association for the Study of the Feebleminded. Meeting attendees adopted a classification system based on an adult's mental age: idiots had mental ages less than two, imbeciles three to seven, and morons eight to twelve. While the term was originally medical in nature, it was "later used to per-petuate negative stereotypes about people with mental retar-dation"[32] and is no longer considered an appropriate term in everyday conversation. It is also no longer used as a psycho-logical classification. However, when *Flowers for Algernon* was written, the term "moron" not only was used popularly to ridicule a person of lower intelligence but was still an accept-ed classification of the mentally challenged.

More complex classification methods followed. Intelligence quotient (IQ) tests were first introduced in 1916 to the United States through the publication of revisions to a French test called the Binet-Simon test. By the time *Flowers for Algernon* was written, other IQ tests had been introduced. The tests were administered widely throughout the United States to classify the mental ages of many citizens, not only the mentally challenged.

Keyes also drew on other psychological tools popular at the time. Early in the novel, Burt Seldon administers a Rorschach test in which Charlie must look at abstract inkblots and report what he sees. Hermann Rorschach first publicized

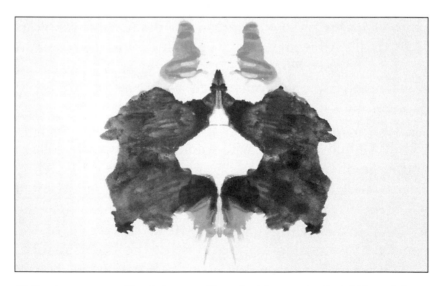

Following surgery, Charly is now able to find images in the inkblots of the Rorschach test, demonstrating to the doctors his new intellectual skills.

that test in 1921 for use in assessing personality traits and psychological conflicts. In the novel, Charlie cannot, at first, imagine any scenes in the inkblots, but after the surgery, he can interpret the images. This change is viewed by the scientists as an indication that Charlie's intelligence is increasing.

While IQ tests and the Rorschach test are used to compare Charlie's intellect and personality before and after the surgery, his personal psychological growth results, in large part, from therapy sessions he undergoes with Dr. Strauss. Dr. Strauss uses a kind of therapy called psychoanalysis that was developed by Sigmund Freud, an Austrian physician born in 1856. In Freud's method, the doctor (a psychoanalyst) encourages the patient to "say everything that comes to mind."[33] Through this technique, called free association, the patient becomes aware of previously unrecognized childhood feelings and memories that influence behavior, self-esteem, and relationships. Charlie explains this process of reaching the unconscious part of the mind in an early progress report:

> I had a nightmare last night, and this morning, after I woke up, I free-associated the way Dr. Strauss told me to do when I remember my dreams. Think about the dream and just let my mind wander until other thoughts come up in my mind. I keep on doing that until my mind goes blank. Dr. Strauss says that it means I've reached a point where my subconscious [unconscious] is trying to block my conscious from remembering. It's a wall between the present and the past. Sometimes the wall stays up and sometimes it breaks down and I can remember what's behind it.[34]

The Rights of the Mentally Challenged

Charlie's psychoanalysis leads him to many important insights. One such insight is that the mentally challenged deserve to be treated with dignity. Society as a whole was coming to this same conclusion around the time that *Flowers for Algernon* was written. Followers of the nineteenth-century evolutionary theories of Charles Darwin had insisted that the mentally challenged be separated from society. As a recent author on the subject explained, "According to some people's views, allowing individuals with mental retardation to mix freely with other members of society interfered with the process of natural selection."[35] The mentally challenged were routinely institutionalized, often in facilities that did little to promote their well-being. Those who lived with their families were kept home from school or placed in regular classes where they could not compete.

The notion that the mentally handicapped could benefit from individualized instruction, geared to an individual's level of development, and that a stimulating environment could raise IQ, were discussed by theorists in the first several decades of the twentieth century. Still, until the 1940s and 1950s, when parents of the mentally challenged organized and established the National Association for Retarded Children (today called the Arc of the United States), few improvements were made. As a result of the association's efforts, Americans became increasingly aware of the needs and problems of the mentally retarded. In 1961, President Kennedy established the President's Panel on Mental Retardation, which recommended the expansion of services to the mentally retarded. By 1975, legislation now called the Individuals with Disabilities Education Act or IDEA, passed. If Keyes had written his book after enactment of that law, he might have dealt with its requirement that mentally retarded students like Charlie be provided a public education appropriate to their individual needs.

Science Fiction Reflects the Times

Keyes used the events of his time to add depth to the novel *Flowers for Algernon*. When Charlie's story is finished, the reader is left to wonder at the mixed blessings of our modern scientific age, and to ask how mentally challenged individuals should be treated.

CHAPTER THREE

Charlie's Journey—A Plot Summary

Flowers for Algernon portrays the personal journey of Charlie Gordon, a mentally retarded man who submits to experimental surgery to increase his intelligence. Charlie describes his journey in progress reports that scientists assign him to write so they will have a record of the outcome of the surgery. The novel takes place in the middle of the twentieth century, when psychiatric classifications label Charlie, whose intelligence quotient (IQ) is only 68, a "moron." While that term is no longer used, it once referred to an adult with a mental age of eight to twelve years. After the surgery, at the height of his brilliance, Charlie's IQ is 185, making him far more intelligent than the scientists who performed the operation.

To Charlie's surprise, intelligence alone does not make him happy and well-adjusted. He suffers emotionally because he now realizes that his family, classmates, and coworkers were cruel to him when he was retarded. He observes the selfish motivations of those around him and becomes increasingly disillusioned with society. Still, he is profoundly disappointed when he finds out that the experiment is destined to fail. He desperately wants to hold on to his new self. His later progress reports convey anger, frustration, and fear as his brilliance slips away.

Charlie Is Selected for the Experiment

The sad tone of Charlie's final reports is markedly different from the tone of the early reports. In the first progress report, long before Charlie understands the consequences of his words, he writes, "I want to be smart."[36] From the beginning, the reader understands how motivated Charlie is. Even before he started writing the progress reports, Charlie showed his motivation in classes taught by Miss Alice Kinnian, a night-school teacher at the Beekman College Center for Retarded Adults in New York City. Because of his positive attitude, Miss Kinnian recommends Charlie for experimental surgery.

The experimental surgery is to be supervised by two scientists, Dr. Jay Strauss, a psychiatrist and neurosurgeon at the Beekman Neuropsychiatric Center, and Professor Harold Nemur, chairman of the Psychology Department at Beekman University. Using a grant from the Welberg Foundation, the two men have successfully increased the intelligence of a mouse named Algernon. The men are seeking a human subject and ask Charlie to write the progress reports so they can decide if they should use him in the experiment.

Charlie is also evaluated with standard personality tests administered by Burt Seldon, Nemur's assistant. One test, the Rorschach, requires Charlie to view inkblots on cards and describe what he sees. He cannot visualize any images and is instead preoccupied by memories of being punished for spilling ink. Charlie is also asked to "race" against Algernon, who has learned to run through different mazes to get food. Charlie is given an electric wand to trace a maze matching Algernon's. The mouse, however, wins again and again.

Charlie overhears the scientists expressing concern about using him for the experiment. Charlie writes, "Prof Nemur

At home, Charly follows the scientists' instructions to "race" against Algernon by tracing an identical maze.

was worryd about my eye-Q getting too high from mine that was too low and I would get sick from it."[37] But, believing they cannot find another retarded man as cooperative and eager to learn, the scientists select Charlie. They temper what Charlie sees as wonderful news by warning him that they cannot predict how a human will react to the experiment and cannot guarantee that any change will be permanent. But Charlie does not hear their concerns. He is convinced that intelligence will change his life, helping him make new friends and assuring him the approval of his family.

A Secret Operation

Charlie takes time off from work as janitor at Donner's Bakery, but he is not permitted to tell anyone that he is undergoing surgery to make him more intelligent. The operation is performed without complications, but when Charlie awakens he tells his nurse, Hilda, that he is disappointed he does not feel smarter. He describes her response in a progress report: "[S]he said mabey they got no rite to make me smart because if god wantid me to be smart he would have made me born that way. And what about Adem and Eev and the sin with the tree of nowlege and eating the appel and the fall. And mabey Prof Nemur and Dr Strauss was tampiring with things they got no rite to tampir with."[38]

Miss Kinnian has a less philosophical explanation for the fact that Charlie does not feel different. She tells Charlie that he needs to work hard to take advantage of his increased mental capability. Disappointed by this reality but still determined, Charlie follows the instructions of the scientists who tell him to play a special television while he sleeps. The television helps him learn subliminally and jogs his memory of childhood events. He also studies reading and writing with Miss Kinnian. Once Charlie beats Algernon at the maze for the first time, signs of increasing intelligence come in quick succession. He reads a

Frustrated by not feeling smarter after the surgery, Charly studies reading and writing with Miss Kinnian to increase his intellect.

novel and grasps grammar and spelling. His progress reports become longer, more thoughtful, and better written.

Change Causes Conflict at the Bakery

Charlie's mental development outstrips his emotional development, causing difficult changes in his relationships. He has worked at Donner's Bakery for seventeen years, since Uncle Herman made the arrangements with Arthur Donner, Herman's good friend. Having the job has allowed Charlie to live outside the Warren State Home, where his parents committed him. Charlie liked his job, perhaps because he never understood that his coworkers were using him as the butt of cruel jokes.

But Charlie is smarter than he used to be. When his coworkers, Frank Reilly, Joe Carp, and Gimpy set him up for an April fool's joke involving what they assume will be his inability to handle the dough machine, Charlie fools everyone by showing that he can, in fact, learn this new skill. This earns him a promotion, but instead of celebrating his success, Frank and Joe resent him and play another cruel trick. They take him to a party, pour alcohol in his drink, and introduce him to a woman named Ellen. When he tries to dance with Ellen, they repeatedly trip him and everyone laughs. Charlie has a painful but important insight: "I never knew before that Joe and Frank and the others liked to have me around just to make fun of me. Now I know what they mean when they say 'to pull a Charlie Gordon.' I'm ashamed."[39]

Fallen Heroes

Charlie's relationships at Beekman College also become more difficult. He asks challenging questions of the scientists and Miss Kinnian, showing that he has reached a mental level that allows him to question authority. When he asks for an explanation of IQ tests, which he was given before the experiment began and which classified him as having low intelligence, he finds that even experts disagree:

Prof. Nemur said it was something that measured how intelligent you were—like a scale in the drugstore weighs pounds. But Dr. Strauss had a big argument with him and said an I.Q. didn't *weigh* intelligence at all. He said an I.Q. showed how much intelligence you could get, like the numbers on the outside of a measuring cup. You still had to fill the cup up with stuff.

When I asked Burt Seldon, who gives me my intelligence tests and works with Algernon, he said that some people would say both of them were wrong and according to the things he's been reading up on, the I.Q. measures a lot of different things including some of the things you learned already and it really isn't a good measure of intelligence at all."[40]

Charlie also questions the value of the personality tests. The next time he is given a Rorschach test, he explodes with anger and accuses Burt of using the cards to make fun of him. When Charlie sees the reaction of the scientists, he knows they recognize an important change in him: "They knew what was happening to me. I had reached a new level, and anger and suspicion were my first reactions to the world around me."[41] When Charlie finally settles down and looks at the Rorschach cards, he sees images. Even this success does not renew his trust in Burt.

Charlie is further confounded by conflicts between the scientists. He overhears Nemur and Strauss arguing about when to present results of the experiment to the scientific community. Nemur wants to present their case at an important conference taking place in Chicago in six weeks. Strauss believes that since Charlie is still changing, they should wait. The argument is heated. "They called each other names—*opportunist, cynic, pessimist*—and I found myself frightened. . . . I was seeing them clearly for the first time—not gods or even heroes, but just two men worried about getting something out of their work."[42]

Charlie tries to find other intellectual companions. He makes friends with the Beekman College students he once observed with envy and listens to their conversations about religion, literature, and philosophy. When someone suggests there is no God, Charlie is frightened because he never before thought to question the existence of God. He begins to think differently about the college education he envied. "Now I understand one of the important reasons for going to college and getting an education is to learn that the things you've believed in all your life aren't true, and that nothing is what it appears to be."[43]

Moral Dilemmas

Charlie's disillusionment with Strauss and Nemur does not prevent him from realizing that eavesdropping on their argument was wrong. That ethical insight is followed by Charlie's first significant moral dilemma. He sees Gimpy pocketing change at the bakery and realizes he has been stealing from Mr. Donner for years. He does not know whether to tell Mr. Donner and worries what will happen if he does. How will Mr. Donner react? If he fires Gimpy, how will Gimpy, a man with a clubfoot, support three children? Relying on Miss Kinnian's advice to trust his instincts, Charlie lets Gimpy know what he has seen. Gimpy has no choice but to stop, satisfying Charlie but leaving him to wonder about the nature of mankind.

A Hole to the Past

To help Charlie cope with the emotional changes, Strauss begins psychotherapy. He assures Charlie that he will someday understand his past, but emphasizes he must first remember childhood events. He asks Charlie to free-associate after dreaming, keeping a record of all the thoughts that come to him. Charlie complies and experiences the sensation that a "hole" has opened in his mind, allowing him to access memories once hidden in his subconscious.

Charlie's memories are vivid and painful, causing him to question his earlier blind trust in people. In one, he is eleven years old and eager to give a valentine to Harriet, a girl who is nice to him. But Charlie knows he lacks the skill to write out his thoughts and asks a classmate to do it for him. In a cruel joke, the classmate writes offensive words on the valentine, with the result that Harriet's brothers beat up Charlie.

Charlie's family memories are vague at first, including only the name of his mother, Rose, and father, Matt, but he soon recalls conflicts between them. Matt and Rose had terrible fights because his mother refused to accept that Charlie would never be normal. Matt was furious that Rose wasted money on experts who made fake promises to change Charlie. Charlie was afraid of his mother and would sometimes express his emotions by losing control of his bowel movements. She would spank him, and although Matt disapproved of her behavior, he would walk away instead of helping Charlie. Charlie now understands that a search for his mother's love is the root of his powerful motivation to learn.

Someone to Love

For the first time, Charlie appreciates that he was, and is, a person who needs someone to love. He finally asks Alice out. They go to the movies, where Charlie experiences an intense physical attraction to her. "I didn't see much of the first picture because I was too conscious of her sitting next to me. Twice her bare arm touched mine on the armrest, and both times the fear that she would become annoyed made me pull back. All I could think about was her soft skin just inches away."[44]

These feelings make him anxious and afraid. He begins to imagine that a young disapproving Charlie is watching them. When he takes Alice to an outdoor concert and puts his arm around her, the imaginary boy looks so real that Charlie jumps up to chase him away.

Charlie's understanding of his sexual fears comes slowly, beginning with a memory of a scene with his mother and his younger sister, Norma. He sees himself as a young boy, looking through a keyhole at Norma bathing. As he wonders why her body is different from his, his mother finds him. Exploding with rage, Rose chases him away at knife-point.

Rejection and Despair

As Charlie struggles to re-solve his fears and become closer to Alice, the crisis at work comes to a head. His coworkers get up a petition and have him fired. Mr. Donner feels bad but ratio-nalizes that Charlie is too

Emotionally immature, Charly has problems handling his attraction to Alice Kinnian.

smart for the job. When Charlie confronts Joe and Frank, they accuse him of arrogance. He believes they hate him because his brilliance makes them feel inadequate.

Only his coworker Fanny Birden refuses to sign the peti-tion. But she scolds him for his ambition to become smart. Like Hilda, the nurse in the hospital, she believes that man should not quest for more than he was given by God. She reminds him how Adam and Eve brought evil into the world by eating from the tree of knowledge.

Charlie is profoundly frustrated by his situation. "This intelligence has driven a wedge between me and all the people I knew and loved, driven me out of the bakery. Now, I'm more alone than ever before. I wonder what would happen if they put Algernon back in the big cage with some of the other mice. Would *they* turn against him?"[45]

Even Charlie and Alice drift apart, partly because of his sexual fears and partly because he is so brilliant that she feels

43

lost talking to him. The experiment is in turmoil too. Strauss and Nemur become increasingly nervous about their decision to present findings at the Chicago conference. They want more reports from Charlie, but he is so engrossed in discovering himself that he finds writing the reports a burden and stops for a while.

Algernon and Charlie Escape

Confirming everyone's worst fears, the conference is a disaster. Charlie embarrasses Nemur in front of his associates by talking about scientific articles written in Hindi, one of many languages Charlie has learned that Nemur does not know. Burt scolds Charlie for his lack of tolerance, and tries to explain that intellectuals are threatened by Charlie's amazing capabilities. But Charlie is disgusted that the men he thought were geniuses are not. He also worries that his fate is in the hands of men who do not have all the answers.

During the presentation of the case, Charlie sits on stage with Algernon, who has been brought along to demonstrate his maze-running abilities. Charlie becomes more and more resentful as the scientists refer to Charlie as a mistake of nature from which they created a genius. He is profoundly hurt and humiliated when the audience laughs at films of the old Charlie trying to beat Algernon in the maze. Charlie feels trapped and identifies with Algernon, who is becoming increasingly agitated.

The information Charlie gains from the presentations disturbs him. For the first time he learns that Algernon's behavior has grown erratic, even in the lab. Using his superior analytical ability, Charlie interprets Strauss and Nemur's data and realizes they have miscalculated the waiting period necessary to prove the experiment is permanent. The significance of this mistake—the near certainty that Charlie will slip back to ignorance—devastates him.

Feeling trapped and furious, Charlie cannot resist the urge to escape. As if in a dream, he unlatches Algernon's cage, setting the mouse loose among the scientists. In the chaos that follows, Charlie recovers Algernon, tucks him neatly in his pocket, and walks out of the convention hall. Knowing he has little time, he flies back to New York, determined to find his parents.

Charlie and Algernon on Their Own

Once he is back, Charlie does not contact anyone from Beekman. He moves to a new apartment, where he builds Algernon a maze. Charlie keeps mostly to himself until he meets Fay Lillman, an artist living next door, who flirts with him. Charlie finds her free spirit attractive.

Charlie tracks down his father, who now lives alone and owns a barbershop. Hoping Matt will recognize him, Charlie does not reveal who he is and instead pretends to be a customer. Matt cuts Charlie's hair and shaves him without showing any recognition of his son. Disappointed, Charlie keeps up the charade, asking to lie under the tanning lamp. There he recalls Matt's betrayal. He imagines himself awakening as a teenager to hear Rose hysterically screaming. She is demanding that Charlie be sent away so Norma can have a normal life. Against his judgment, Matt gives in and takes Charlie to the Warren State Home. Charlie's memory makes him physically ill. Feeling foolish for seeking the approval of a man who hurt him and does not even remember him, Charlie leaves the barbershop without revealing his identity.

Charlie turns to Fay for comfort, but he cannot make love to her because of the continuing psychological fear his mother will punish him. To escape his emotional pain, he goes on what he describes as an anti-intellectual binge. He wanders the streets of New York, attends western and horror movies, and finally ends up in a diner. There he watches as a mentally retarded busboy drops a tray of glasses. Everyone laughs at the boy, including Charlie. Charlie is furious with himself for reacting the way the crowd does.

The event has great significance for Charlie, because it reminds him that he is not the only mentally retarded person with problems. He resolves to use his limited time to help the 5 million mentally retarded Americans and asks the Welberg Foundation for permission to do independent work on the project.

But Charlie's work is interrupted by his continuing search for human affection. He visits Alice and tells her he longs to find an emotional connection with others that will allow him to keep his intellectual freedom. They try to make love, but Charlie cannot. He finds that he can ignore the imaginary Charlie only with Fay, for whom he has no love. He begins a sexual relationship with Fay, and they spend long nights club hopping and drinking alcohol.

The "Algernon-Gordon Effect"

Charlie's escape from reality ends abruptly when he sees that Algernon—whom he has been keeping as a pet—is quickly deteriorating. He returns to Beekman and learns more painful lessons. Research into current psychology theories brings him to conclude they are based on "wishful thinking" about human intelligence, memory, and learning. In his analysis of the experiment, presented in his report called "The Algernon-Gordon Effect," Charlie states that his artificially induced intelligence will deteriorate. Sadly, he also concludes that the larger the increase of intelligence, the faster the deterioration. When Algernon dies, dissection of the animal's brain confirms Charlie's hypothesis.

One question remains: What should be done with the subjects of the failed experiment? When Charlie learns he will probably live in the Warren State Home, he muses that at least he will not be incinerated like the animal subjects. He rescues Algernon from this fate and buries him in his backyard. He then visits the institution from which Uncle Herman and Mr. Donner rescued him seventeen years earlier. Seeing the empty expressions of the residents, he characterizes Warren as a home for the living dead. He holds out hope that he can avoid moving there, in spite of the emotional changes brought on by the experiment.

A Final Quest

Charlie's ordeal has taught him that learning and intelligence must be tempered by human affection or moral breakdown will occur. His relationship with Alice is his one chance for human affection, but he knows he must resolve childhood fears before he can become close to Alice. He visits his mother, whose senility makes her mind wander, but who finally recognizes him and reluctantly lets him into her house. When he explains he is smart, she is overjoyed. For the first time in his life, he brings a smile to her lips.

Norma, who lives with Rose, is glad to see her older brother. She explains how she gave consent for his operation and read about him in the paper. She confesses that when they were kids she hated him because of ridicule she suffered at school. She feels bad that Rose sent him away because of an unfounded belief that Charlie would harm Norma. Norma guiltily confesses that she had lied to Rose about Charlie's hurting her.

Weary of caring for Rose, Norma begs Charlie to stay. When he offers to send money but says he must go, she clings to him. Believing he has made a sexual overture to Norma, Rose threatens Charlie with a knife. Through this reenactment of childhood events, Charlie understands the basis of his sexual fears.

The Sad Goodbye

Charlie and Alice finally make love. But their emotional connection is soon shattered. Aware of his mental decline, Charlie holes up in his room. He tries to read but can no longer understand books he enjoyed a short time before. He destroys them and his classical music records and becomes furious when Alice tries to clean up the mess. When she scolds him for watching television and wallowing in self-pity, he becomes furious and accuses, "You keep pretending I can do things and understand things that are far beyond me now. You're pushing me. Just like my mother."[46] Finally, he asks her to leave and refuses contact with her or anyone from Beekman.

Charlie tries to fit in again at the bakery. But even though Joe, Frank, and Gimpy are nice to him now, he cannot handle the ridicule of a new worker. Searching for his place in society, he returns to the class for retarded adults, forgetting that he is no longer enrolled. When Alice sees him, she bursts into tears and runs from the classroom. While he no longer understands the complexity of Alice's feelings, he knows he has made a mistake. He realizes that he might make other hurtful mistakes and decides to go to the Warren House to live.

In the last progress report, Charlie says goodbye to Alice and Dr. Strauss and gently urges Professor Nemur not to be a grouch. Finally, he writes, "please if you get a chanse put some flowrs on Algernons grave in the bak yard."[47]

CHAPTER FOUR

The Characters

Each of the characters in *Flowers for Algernon* plays an important role in defining the themes of the story. Secondary characters also help the reader understand the main characters. By seeing the way Charlie reacts to Algernon, Alice, Nemur, his parents, and coworkers, and how they treat and react to him, the reader can better understand why Charlie behaves and feels as he does. Because the other characters are all described in Charlie's words, details such as their ages and physical descriptions are sometimes not provided. Nevertheless, each character exhibits human traits the reader can recognize and form opinions about. In this way, the story makes the reader think about the issues and themes that were important to Keyes.

Algernon

The white mouse, Algernon, is an experimental animal made smarter by the same type of surgery that is later performed on Charlie. Because Algernon shows exceptional abilities after the operation, Dr. Strauss and Professor Nemur are emboldened to test their results on a human subject.

As test subjects, Algernon and Charlie exhibit similarities. On the first page of the novel, for example, Charlie describes a long hall lined with little rooms where he is taken for personality tests. Algernon's intelligence testing takes place in a maze that is remarkably similar. Likewise, Charlie and Algernon are encouraged to participate in the experiment by real or perceived rewards. Algernon's reward for running the maze is food. Charlie assumes (mistakenly) that he will win the approval and affection of his family and friends. As Charlie learns, these human rewards are no less crucial to his survival than food is to Algernon's.

At the outset of the novel, both subjects are trapped, Algernon in his cages and mazes and Charlie by society's perception of him as less than human. Both finally rebel against the insensitive treatment they receive, with Charlie masterminding their escape from the scientific convention. When the tests fail, Algernon and Charlie are pushed aside as if they were inanimate objects in a chemistry experiment.

By naming the book *Flowers for Algernon*, Keyes highlights its tragic structure. Charlie can predict his future by watching Algernon's decline and eventual death. Charlie, too, loses everything, but in the human sense of loss: he must spend the rest of his life at the Warren Home, an institution for the mentally retarded where, he observes, "[t]he feeling was of living death— or worse, of never having been fully alive and knowing."[48]

In many ways, Algernon is the most important character besides Charlie. The mouse is the one creature that expects nothing from Charlie. Because of this, no matter how arrogant or embittered Charlie becomes, he never loses sympathy or compassion for Algernon. Thus, the interaction between Charlie and Algernon shows readers the most human side of Charlie; he is, indeed, capable of great emotional pain. And when Charlie grieves for his "friend" by laying flowers on his grave, he is also grieving for himself.

Fanny Birden

Fanny, Charlie's coworker at the bakery, is a little-seen but important character. First, she is the only person who takes seriously Charlie's desire to read. When he asks how he can learn, she refers him to the Beekman College classes for retarded adults. Charlie's attendance at the school is an

Highly motivated to learn all he can, Charly attends college classes for retarded adults at the recommendation of his coworker, Fanny.

important plot point: it puts him in contact with Miss Kinnian, who recommends him for the experiment. Charlie's enrollment at night school also shows the reader that he is a character who is highly motivated to improve himself.

Fanny is also important because she gives voice to a central theme of the book. When Charlie explains that an operation made him smart, she replies, "If you'd read your Bible, Charlie, you'd know that it's not meant for man to know more than was given to him to know by the Lord in the first place."[49] Her comment causes Charlie and the reader to consider the moral dimension of using science to "improve" human intelligence.

Joe Carp

Joe is a coworker at the bakery who participates in playing cruel jokes on Charlie. In one stunt, after Charlie's operation, Joe asks

Charlie if he would like to work the dough mixer, assuming Charlie will make a fool of himself because he will not be able to follow instructions on how to operate the machine. However, Charlie, benefiting from his increasing intellect, figures out the machine and ends up getting a promotion. This event sets the stage for a dramatic shift in Charlie's role at Donner's Bakery. When Charlie demonstrates he has developed the ability to learn the machine, his coworkers feel threatened. Soon after, Joe and the other workers rally successfully to have Charlie fired.

But by the end of the story, when Charlie returns to the bakery in his regressed state, Joe stands up for Charlie. When Klaus, a new worker, ridicules Charlie, Joe comes to his defense, insisting that "Charlie is a good guy and nobody's gonna start up with him without answering for it."[50] Thus, Joe has come to see the humanity in a man he once considered worthy only of ridicule.

Arthur Donner

Arthur Donner owns Donner's Bakery, where Charlie has worked for seventeen years. A friend of Charlie's Uncle Herman, Mr. Donner has kept Charlie employed and out of the Warren Home for all of Charlie's adult life.

Unfortunately, Mr. Donner does not remain loyal to Charlie. Like others in Charlie's life, Mr. Donner caves in to pressure from people who do not have Charlie's interests in mind. When the bakery workers complain that the changes in Charlie make them uncomfortable, Mr. Donner fires Charlie, rationalizing his action by claiming that Charlie, who has the Beekman Institute's support, no longer needs a job.

In the conversation in which he fires Charlie, Mr. Donner insists, "I treated you like my own son."[51] The comment is ironic on two levels. First, Mr. Donner is not protecting Charlie the way a father would, and second, Charlie's real father also banished Charlie, in that case from his home. When Mr. Donner takes Charlie back after his intellect has regressed, his kindness

Although Charly had worked for years at Donner's Bakery, Mr. Donner bows to pressure from Charly's coworkers and fires him.

is tinged by self-interest; Charlie, once again retarded, no longer creates problems for Mr. Donner.

Gimpy

Gimpy was given his nickname because he has a clubfoot. The head baker at Donner's, Gimpy often yells at Charlie, but can also be kind. Once, after the retarded Charlie is humiliated trying to learn to make rolls, Gimpy comforts him by giving him a brass disc Charlie believes is a good-luck medal.

But Gimpy has another side, one that challenges Charlie to make the first self-conscious moral decision of his life. Gimpy is dishonest. For years he has been skimming cash from Mr. Donner's register. Charlie's realization of this is a milestone in his intellectual growth. First, it shows a heightened understanding of the significance of events. Second, it exemplifies a heightened moral sensitivity.

Once Charlie acknowledges the dishonest action, he cannot ignore it. He feels that Gimpy has betrayed Mr. Donner.

At the same time, Gimpy has been kinder to Charlie than some people, and Charlie sympathizes with the man because he, too, has a disability that could make finding another job difficult. Charlie is all the more concerned because Gimpy is the father of three children who rely on him for support.

Charlie cleverly stops Gimpy's stealing by suggesting that someone might tell Mr. Donner about the stealing if it continues. Trapped, Gimpy stops the illegal behavior but harbors enough anger to participate in the petition to fire Charlie. Later, though, when Charlie is forced to return to the bakery, Gimpy is kinder, even defending Charlie when Klaus, the new worker, is mean.

Charlie Gordon

Charlie, the main character in the novel, is a thirty-two-year-old, mentally retarded janitor and errand boy at Donner's Bakery. He attends night school for retarded adults at Beekman College. Banished from his home as a teenager, he has lived alone and worked at Donner's Bakery for seventeen years. He hangs around socially with coworkers, but only because they want someone to tease. His parents and younger sister, Norma, have not seen him in years.

A joyful Charly, depicted here, soon finds that his increased intelligence leads to heartache and disillusion.

Charlie is profoundly naïve at first. He mistakes his coworkers' cruel jokes for friendship. He also trusts that changing his brain by surgery will bring him immediate rewards of brilliance and happiness.

But he soon learns he must struggle to grow smart, and that being smart leads him to remember and understand events that cause emotional pain. Increased intelligence also means having responsibility to make moral decisions, for example, whether to report Gimpy for stealing. He also develops a desire to have a special relationship with a woman, which he tries to achieve, without success, with Miss Kinnian.

Charlie's personal journey is primarily one of self-discovery. Other than the operation, few dramatic events occur in his life. Through the teachings of Miss Kinnian and his psychotherapy with Dr. Strauss, he develops from a man who is naïve, ignorant, and childlike to one who is intellectually brilliant but emotionally immature.

Charlie's kind nature lurks beneath the anguished, arrogant genius portrayed in the middle parts of the novel. When he sinks back into mental retardation, he no longer undestands difficult intellectual material. But he has retained enough of his emotional development to recognize that his presence in Miss Kinnian's classroom is painful to her. In response, he decides to go to the Warren Home, a place where no one will pity him.

Matt Gordon

Charlie's father, a barber, is one of many people in Charlie's life who are not necessarily mean-spirited but who do not have the courage to stand up for Charlie. In contrast to Charlie's mother, Rose, who seeks to improve Charlie and make him more acceptable to society, Matt accepts Charlie's disability. Matt goes through the motions of demanding that Rose and Charlie's sister, Norma, be nice to Charlie. But at the crucial moment when Rose hysterically demands that Charlie be sent away, Matt gives in with barely a protest and takes Charlie away.

Matt eventually leaves Rose, but he makes no effort to find his son and reconcile with him. In fact, Matt thinks so little about Charlie that when the intellectual Charlie poses as an anonymous barbershop customer, Matt does not realize he is cutting his son's hair. This scene leads to some of Charlie's bitterest thoughts. After finally admitting to himself that his father does not recognize him, Charlie thinks, "How absurd I was sitting in his shop, waiting for him to pat me on the head and say, 'Good boy.'"[52]

Norma Gordon

Norma is Charlie's younger sister, who falsely claimed that Charlie hurt her as a child, leading to Charlie's removal from the family. Norma endured ridicule from classmates because of Charlie's limitations and retaliated by telling people he was not her real brother. Norma's actions, remembered by the intelligent Charlie in psychotherapy, hurt him deeply. But Norma seems more like a spoiled child who received little guidance about dealing with her unusual brother than a deliberately cruel person. Norma plays an important role in Charlie's adult life because she gives consent for Charlie's participation in the experiment. Until the scientists approach her with the consent form, she believes, from what her parents said, that Charlie is dead.

Norma sees Charlie as an adult for the first time when he visits their mother. Norma does not have clear memories of their childhood difficulties. She is especially delighted to see Charlie since he now has the mental capacity to play the role of older brother, which would be helpful in dealing with their senile mother. When Charlie says he cannot stay, Norma clings to him, causing their mother to fly into a rage and threaten Charlie with a knife. That incident, and Norma's confession that she lied to their mother about Charlie's childhood behavior, help Charlie understand why he is afraid of women.

Rose Gordon

Charlie's mother, whom he has not seen in years, is the most influential person in his life. Through psychotherapy, the intelligent

Charlie realizes that he is driven to be smart because he always believed that would be the one way to win Rose's love and approval. When Charlie was a child, Rose was preoccupied with "curing" Charlie of his mental retardation and dragged him to doctors, who falsely promised cures. She was often harsh with Charlie, beating him and chasing him with a knife because she feared that Charlie had a sexual interest in Norma. To protect Norma, Rose insisted that Charlie be removed from their home.

While Rose figures prominently in Charlie's growing store of recovered memories, as an adult he sees her in person only once. She has become senile and at first does not recognize her son. She finally realizes, for one brief moment, that he is smart. That moment is one of the most poignant in the book because it highlights the emotional deprivation Charlie suffered: "She hugged me, talking excitedly, making plans for the new life we were going to have together. . . . For the first time in my life, I had brought a smile to her lips."[53]

Charlie's fear of women stems from his mother's rejection of him. Rose's behavior was caused partly by her drive for perfection (including a desire to impress the neighbors). But her most violent reactions, including her banishment of Charlie when he was only fifteen years old, were caused by Rose's misperception that Charlie was acting sexually toward his sister. Once Charlie sees his mother and realizes that her behavior was irrational and cruel, rather than a true indication of his worth as a human being, he is able to become emotionally involved with Alice.

Uncle Herman

Uncle Herman, an overweight housepainter, took Charlie in when Rose and Matt kicked him out of their home. Herman died just two years later, when Charlie was seventeen, but he played a crucial role in assuring that Charlie would not have to live at the Warren Home; through Herman's arrangement with Mr. Donner, Charlie maintained his independence.

Nurse Hilda

Hilda, Charlie's "skinney" nurse after surgery, plays only one role in the novel: she, like Fanny Birden, expresses the view that perhaps Charlie should have accepted the limitations God gave him. Her doubts foreshadow Charlie's decline.

Alice Kinnian

Alice Kinnian, Charlie's teacher in night school, is impressed by his gentle nature and eagerness to learn. She urges Dr. Strauss and Professor Nemur to use Charlie for the experiment. Alice, as Charlie comes to call her, is pretty, emotional, and caring. She teaches Charlie after the surgery and helps him attain superintelligence, then falls in love with the man she has helped create. Charlie falls in love with her too, describing her in a report about their first date as having "pigeon-soft brown eyes and feathery brown hair down to the hollow of her neck. When she smiles, her full lips look as if she's pouting."[54] Unfortunately, before long, Alice is overwhelmed by Charlie's unnatural brilliance and complicated emotional problems.

Charly's love interest, Alice Kinnian, helps guide Charly through his progression from child to adolescent to man.

Alice is Charlie's emotional and romantic mentor, ushering him through his rapid growth from child to adolescent to man. Alice's affection motivates Charlie to understand his problems with his mother, which is crucial to his overcoming a fear of love and sexual intimacy. Through their lovemaking, Alice helps

Charlie understand the fundamental importance of human affection.

Unfortunately, Alice cannot save Charlie from his intellectual slide. Grief-stricken and plagued by guilt, she cannot handle seeing him after his decline, a fact that makes Charlie decide to go into the Warren Home.

Fay Lillman

After Charlie leaves the scientists' convention with Algernon in his pocket, he goes into hiding in a new apartment in New York City. There he meets Fay, a slender, blonde, free-spirited artist who lives next door and climbs through Charlie's living room window for visits. Her disordered, Bohemian lifestyle appeals to Charlie at a time when he is feeling confined by his role as experimental subject. She provides an escape from his troubles and the heavy responsibility of discovering why the experiment failed. They spend evenings dancing and drinking. Charlie has his first sexual experience with Fay, preparing him to make love to Alice, the woman he truly loves.[55]

Although Fay never knows the real Charlie, she intuitively senses his loneliness. When she brings Algernon a female mouse for companionship, Charlie thinks, "I'm glad that Algernon is no longer alone."[55]

Professor Harold Nemur

Professor Nemur, chairman of the Psychology Department at Beekman University, has a great deal riding on the success of Charlie's surgery. His research is conducted with a grant from the prestigious Welberg Foundation, meaning he will suffer terrible embarrassment in the scientific community if the experiment fails. He is also pushed by his wife to succeed. Because of the pressure, Nemur is capable of terrible insensitivity, for example, when he speaks of Charlie in his announcement at the convention: "We who have worked on this project at Beekman University have the satisfaction of knowing we have taken one of nature's mistakes and by our new techniques created a superior human being."[56] Professor Nemur's treatment of Charlie presents an important theme, expressed by Charlie when he tells Nemur, "But I'm not an inanimate object. I'm a *person*."[57] In other words, Charlie is insisting that all people, regardless of their limitations, should be treated with dignity.

Charlie's contacts with Professor Nemur illuminate and influence Charlie's intellectual journey in several ways. Before the surgery, Charlie buys into Professor Nemur's enthusiasm without questioning his motives or abilities. As Charlie becomes smarter, he begins to realize that Professor Nemur is no god, but instead an ambitious and flawed man. When Charlie is at the peak of his brilliance, he feels contempt for Professor Nemur's more limited intelligence and embarrasses the scientist in front of colleagues at the convention. Finally, Charlie realizes the personal consequences of Professor Nemur's limitations: the experimental data are flawed, meaning Charlie will return to his mentally handicapped state.

Frank Reilly

Charlie's coworker, Frank, is a ladies' man who arranges social events that usually lead to cruel jokes played on Charlie. In one joke, Frank gets Charlie drunk and has him dance with a woman, leading to Charlie's first awareness of his adult sexuality. As Charlie becomes smarter he understands Frank's motivations. This causes emotional pain that contributes to Charlie's bitterness, especially when Charlie realizes Frank has organized the petition drive to get him fired from Donner's Bakery. The fact that Charlie confronts Frank about the petition is a sign of Charlie's increased ability to feel and express moral outrage.

Frank is also important because a comment he makes early in the book foreshadows Charlie's troubles. When Charlie says he is going to study at Beekman night school, Frank jokingly warns, "[D]ont go getting so eddicated that you wont talk to your old frends."[58]

Burt Seldon

Burt is the graduate student assistant who gives Charlie his first personality tests. Burt means well, but he does not effectively handle Charlie's frustration with the tests. Burt participates in the study without considering its ethical implications. He acts as an emotional mentor to Charlie by explaining that Professor Nemur is threatened by Charlie's brilliance. He also encourages Charlie to be less arrogant and more tolerant of those around him.

Burt may be the young man Charlie wished he could have been. During his intellectual decline, Charlie meets with Burt and learns that the young man is finishing his doctoral degree in psychology. The contrast between the two men—one growing intellectually and the other declining—is poignant for Charlie and the reader.

Dr. Jay Strauss

A psychiatrist and neurosurgeon at Beekman Neuropsychiatric Center, Dr. Strauss works with Professor Nemur on the experiment, performing the operation and later acting as Charlie's therapist. In that role, he helps Charlie uncover and grapple with childhood memories and cautions Charlie about the inevitable emotional problems he will have. He reassures Charlie that he will be there to help and stays available to him until Charlie finally pushes everyone away.

Dr. Strauss sees Charlie as a human being and is more protective of his patient's welfare than Professor Nemur. Nevertheless, Dr. Strauss gives in on the key decision of when to release the results of the experiment, leading to the disaster at the convention. Like Professor Nemur, Dr. Strauss does not predict that the experiment will fail.

CHAPTER FIVE

Themes of *Flowers for Algernon*

Unlike some science fiction writers who focus primarily on the technical details of an imaginary scientific event, Keyes uses the experimental surgery as a launching point to explore human character and to pose questions about the ethical use of science to "improve" a person. Several characters—notably Professor Nemur, Dr. Strauss, Miss Kinnian, and Charlie—have high hopes that the experimental brain surgery can make Charlie's life better. Other characters, including Nurse Hilda and Fanny Birden, make religious arguments against the procedure. After witnessing Charlie's ascent to brilliance and his regression to mental retardation, the reader, too, may form opinions about whether it is ethical or proper to use science to "improve" a human being. In addition, the reader may feel sympathy for Charlie, whose need for love and acceptance is thwarted because he and other characters are flawed by human weaknesses such as arrogance, ambition, emotional immaturity, intolerance, and fear.

Loneliness and Isolation

Because human weaknesses make Charlie's connection with other people impossible, he is lonely and isolated. His state of alienation begins before the surgery, increases as he becomes more brilliant, and finally becomes absolute when he takes himself out of society to live at the Warren State Home. Charlie's three stages of isolation are described in the progress reports. From the outset, his observations, although unsophisticated, show that he is aware of being an outsider. "If the operashun werks and I get smart mabye Ill be abel to find my mom and dad and sister and show them. Boy woud they be serprised to see me smart just like them and my sister. . . . I just want to be smart like other pepul so I can have lots of frends who like me."[59] He also writes, "I got to try to be smart like other pepul. Then when I am smart they will talk to me and I can sit with them and listen like Joe Carp and Frank and Gimpy do when they talk and have a discushen about important things."[60]

Insight and Disenchantment

Charlie's growing intellect brings greater insight, as shown through his reaction to one of the first books he reads, *Robinson Crusoe* by Daniel Defoe. Charlie's reaction to the adventures of a man stranded on an island shows his developing sense of the importance of human connection. "Hes smart and figgers out all kinds of things so he can have a house and food and hes a good swimmer. Only I feel sorry for him because hes all alone and he has no frends. . . . I hope he gets a frend and not be so lonely."[61]

In the early stages of Charlie's intellectual ascent, his memories of the cruel behavior of coworkers make him realize the depth of his alienation. In one incident, he literally stands alone after attending a party with coworkers. "[T]hey asked me to go around the corner to see if it was raining and when I came back there was no one their. Maybe they went to find me. I looked for them all over till it was late. . . . Then I dont remember so good but Mrs Flynn says a nice poleecman brought me back home."[62] Even more painful are Charlie's memories of how he was made to feel inadequate in his family. His mother's constant quest to find specialists who could make him more normal, her impatience with his limitations, and her final banishment of him from the family all show a painfully lonely childhood.

In the second stage of Charlie's journey, when he is climbing to and finally reaches the intellectual peak, his alienation and loneliness stem partly from people's reactions to those changes and partly from the way he treats others. After he is fired, Charlie asks Frank why the employees wanted to get rid of him. Frank replies, "Why? I'll tell you why. Because all of a sudden you're a big shot, a know-it-all, a brain! Now you're a regular whiz kid, an egghead. Always with a book—always with all the answers. Well, I'll tell you something. You think you're better than the rest of us here? Okay, go someplace else."[63] Charlie's new behavior threatens people like Frank who used to enjoy feeling superior to him.

A High Price for Arrogance

While Frank is describing what is, at first, Charlie's enthusiasm about his new abilities, Charlie later, at the height of his brilliance, becomes intolerably arrogant. Keyes warns about the dangers of arrogance earlier in the story, in a conversation Charlie has with Alice. Describing her student's future, Alice says, "You'll climb higher and higher to see more and more of the world around you."[64] Alice's remark seems to allude to the Greek mythological figure Icarus, who is often cited as an example of a man punished for arrogance. Imprisoned on an island, Icarus escaped by flying on wax wings, but he ignored his father's warning to maintain a moderate height. Instead, he flew so close to the heat of the sun that his wings melted and he plunged to his death. Like Icarus, Charlie pays a high price in the form of loneliness for his lofty view of the world.

Charlie suffers the consequences of his arrogance—conflicts with the scientists and an inability to bond with Alice—for a long while before he has the insight to realize his flaw. Burt Seldon, the graduate student assistant, helps Charlie toward this understanding, causing Charlie to write, "As shocking as it is to discover the truth about men I had respected and looked up to,

I guess Burt is right. I must not be too impatient with them. Their ideas and brilliant work made the experiment possible. I've got to guard against the natural tendency to look down on them now that I have surpassed them."[65]

Mental Intelligence and Emotional Maturity

Charlie's isolation during this middle stage is also a result of his lack of emotional maturity. While his intellect soars, his emotional maturity, according to one critic, "follows, struggling."[66] Charlie's emotional problems surface early on, as Dr. Strauss warns they will. "[Dr. Strauss] feels that my rapid intellectual development has deceived me into thinking I could live a normal emotional life."[67]

Charlie yearns to overcome his emotional immaturity. "I've got to grow up. For me it means everything,"[68] he laments. He describes his emotional state as one of adolescence that does not allow him to develop a meaningful relationship with Alice: "I wanted to be in love with her. I wanted to overcome my emotional and sexual fears, to marry, have children, settle down."[69]

Charlie's feelings about Alice illustrate his fundamental, but frustrated, need for love. After Alice refuses to let Charlie kiss her, he thinks, "It was wrong for me to express my feelings to Alice. I have no right to think of a woman that way—not yet. But even as I write these words, something inside shouts that there is more. I'm a person. I was somebody before I went under the surgeon's knife. And I have to love someone."[70]

Because he is falling in love with Alice, Charlie is motivated to step off his metaphorical island. To do this he must understand why he fears women. Gradually, he remembers that his mother threatened him for being curious about the physical differences between him and his sister Norma. Unfortunately, his insight into his fears comes too late as Charlie's intellect begins to deteriorate. Charlie's emotional maturity never does catch up. However, there is the lingering sense that if he had been given just a little more time, he and Alice might have developed a mature and meaningful relationship.

Dignity, Humanity, and Respect

While Charlie behaves arrogantly and fails to achieve emotional maturity, those behaviors are not the only cause of his isolation. Because of his disability, others treat him as if he were unworthy of their respect and affection. Critics have found this theme to be clearly and effectively stated in the book. As *New York Times* reviewer Eliot Fremont-Smith notes, "The obvious part is the message: We must respect life, respect one another, be kind to those less fortunate than ourselves."[71] Keyes has also been praised for successfully creating a sympathetic character whose problems lead readers to appreciate that one detail of a person's makeup, his IQ, can lead to profound differences in his treatment by society. As one critic put it, *Flowers for Algernon* should "make us reflect that, but for the grace of God, might we [be in Charlie's shoes]."[72]

Charlie does not realize his low status in society until after the operation, but once he becomes self-aware he rebels against the attitude that the mentally challenged do not deserve respect and kindness. When Charlie develops insight into the human character, he writes: "Even a feeble-minded man wants to be like other men. A child may not know how to feed itself, or what to eat, yet it knows hunger."[73] Charlie uses this metaphor to describe a person's basic need to be cared for as a human being.

At the height of his intellectual powers, Charlie has remarkable insights that bring out this theme. When he catches himself joining in with the crowd and laughing at a mentally challenged busboy for dropping a tray, he realizes how wrong such behavior is. "At first I had been amused along with the rest. Suddenly, I was furious at myself and all those who were smirking at him. . . . I jumped up and shouted: 'Shut up! Leave him alone! He can't understand. He can't help what he is . . . but for God's sake, have some respect! *He's a human being!*"[74]

Later, he confronts Professor Nemur and insists on his own humanity: "Yes, suddenly we discover that I was always a person—even before—and that challenges your belief that someone with an I.Q. of less than 100 doesn't deserve consideration." He also angrily declares to Professor Nemur, "Here in your university, intelligence, education, knowledge, have all become great idols. But I know now there's one thing you've all overlooked: intelligence and education that hasn't been tempered by human affection isn't worth a damn."[75]

Thirst for Knowledge

Keyes has written that Charlie's fall from great human heights "is the major power and structure"[76] of the novel. By writing the story as a tragedy, Keyes considers the dangers of using science to alter human beings. Keyes uses two minor characters, Nurse Hilda and coworker Fanny Birden, to express the notion that altering intelligence may be viewed as sinful. Charlie tells Nurse Hilda that the operation's purpose was to make him smart, then reports her reply: "Mabey they got no rite to make me smart because if god wantid me to be smart he would have made me born that way. And what about Adem and Eev and the sin with the tree of nowlege and eating the appel and the fall. And mabey Prof Nemur and Dr Strauss was tampiring with things they got no rite to tampir with."[77]

Later, Charlie's question sparks another important conversation with Fanny:

> "But what's wrong with a person wanting to be more intelligent, to acquire knowledge, and understand himself and the world?" [Charlie asked.]

> "If you'd read your Bible, Charlie, you'd know that it's not meant for man to know more than was given to him

to know by the Lord in the first place. The fruit of that tree was forbidden to man. . . ."

"There's no going back, Fanny. I haven't done anything wrong. I'm like a man born blind who has been given a chance to see light. That can't be sinful. Soon there'll be millions like me all over the world. Science can do it, Fanny. . . ."

"It was evil when Adam and Eve ate from the *tree of knowledge*. It was evil when they saw they was naked, and learned about lust and shames. And they was driven out of Paradise and the gates was closed to them. If not for that none of us would have to grow old and be sick and die." [78]

Several characters participate in the symbolically described act of "eating from the tree of knowledge," most obviously the scientists who perform the experiment. Professor Nemur describes himself as a creator when he summarizes the results of the experiment at the scientific convention, "We have taken one of nature's mistakes and by our new techniques created a superior human being. . . . It might be said that Charlie Gordon did not really exist before this experiment."[79] Charlie later accuses Nemur of playing God when he says, "You've boasted time and again that I was nothing before the experiment, and I know why. Because if I was nothing, then you were responsible for creating me, and that makes you my lord and master."[80]

Flowers for Algernon has been praised for raising the important issue of the ethical use of science. As one critic suggests, Charlie's "treatment as an object of scientific curiosity throughout his ordeal underlines the book's points about deficiencies in the scientific method as applied to human beings."[81]

Hard Questions

Charlie himself expresses his opinion about the wisdom of pursuing the experiment. Before he suffers the ultimate penalty—banishment to the Warren State Home—he muses on what knowledge means to him. In one report, at the height of his intellectual understanding of the experiment's flaw, he writes, "It's as if all the knowledge I've soaked in during the past months has coalesced and lifted me to a peak of light and understanding. This is beauty, love, and truth all rolled into one. This is joy. And now that I've found it, how can I give it up? Life and work are the most wonderful things a man can have."[82]

Later, he sums up his feelings about the experiment:

I want to say here again what I've said already to Dr. Strauss. No one is in any way to blame for what has happened. This experiment was carefully prepared, extensively tested on animals, and statistically validated. When they decided to use me as the first human test, they were reasonably certain that there was no physical danger involved. There was no way to foresee the psychological pitfalls. I don't want anyone to suffer because of what happens to me.

The only question now is: How much can I hang on to?[83]

Keyes poses questions about human behavior, most fundamentally the consequences of the human quest for knowledge. No clear answers are given, but one is left to ponder his several themes and to consider how things might have turned out better for Charlie or if such experiments should be conducted at all.

Notes

Chapter 1: A Biography of Daniel Keyes

1. Daniel Keyes, *Algernon, Charlie and I: A Writer's Journey*. Boca Raton, FL: Challenge Press, 1999, p. 22.

2. Keyes, *Algernon, Charlie and I*, pp. 61–62.

3. Keyes, *Algernon, Charlie and I*, p. 15.

4. Keyes, *Algernon, Charlie and I*, p. 15.

5. Keyes, *Algernon, Charlie and I*, p. 36.

6. Keyes, *Algernon, Charlie and I*, p. 44.

7. Keyes, *Algernon, Charlie and I*, pp. 44–45.

8. Keyes, *Algernon, Charlie and I*, p. 56.

9. Keyes, *Algernon, Charlie and I*, p. 57.

10. Keyes, *Algernon, Charlie and I*, pp. 69–70.

11. Keyes, *Algernon, Charlie and I*, p. 82.

12. *Locus*, "Daniel Keyes: 40 Years of Algernon," June 1997, p. 5.

13. *Locus*, "Daniel Keyes," p. 5.

14. *Locus*, "Daniel Keyes," p. 5.

15. Keyes, *Algernon, Charlie and I*, p. 87.

16. Keyes, *Algernon, Charlie and I*, p. 14.

17. Keyes, *Algernon, Charlie and I*, p. 66.

18. Keyes, *Algernon, Charlie and I*, p. 35.

19. Hillary Keyes, "The Fifth Sally," http://in.flite.net/~dkeyes/sally.html.

20. Quoted in Anne Commire, ed., "Daniel Keyes," in *Something About the Author*, vol. 37. Detroit, MI: Gale Research, 1985, p. 88.

21. Hillary Keyes, "The Milligan Wars," http://in.flite.net/~dkeyes/milligan.html.

22. Commire, *Something About the Author*, p. 88.

23. Keyes, *Algernon, Charlie and I*, p. 161.

24. Keyes, *Algernon, Charlie and I*, p. 177.

25. *Locus*, "Daniel Keyes," p. 73.

Chapter 2: Science Fiction in a Time of Change

26. Thomas L. Wymer et al., eds., *Intersections: The Elements of Fiction in Science Fiction*. Bowling Green, OH: Popular Press, 1978, p. 4.

27. Peter Nicholls, ed., *The Science Fiction Encyclopedia*. Garden City, NY: Doubleday, 1979, p. 134.

28. John J. Pierce, *Great Themes of Science Fiction: A Study of Imagination and Evolution*. New York: Greenwood Press, 1987, p. 27.

29. Pierce, *Great Themes of Science Fiction*, p. 26.

30. Francis Leone, *Genetics: The Mystery and the Promise*. Blue Ridge Summit, PA: TAB Books, 1992, p. viii.

31. Martin Walker, *The Cold War: A History*. New York: Henry Holt, 1993, p. 171.

32. Romayne Smith, ed., *Children with Mental Retardation: A Parents' Guide*. Rockville, MD: Woodbine House, 1993, p. 45.

33. American Psychoanalytic Association, http://apsa.org/pubinfo/about.htm.

34. Daniel Keyes, *Flowers for Algernon*. New York: Bantam Books, 1975, p. 35.

35. Smith, *Children with Mental Retardation*, p.45

Chapter 3: Charlie's Journey—A Plot Summary

36. Keyes, *Flowers for Algernon*, p. 1.

37. Keyes, *Flowers for Algernon*, p. 7.

38. Keyes, *Flowers for Algernon*, p. 12.

39. Keyes, *Flowers for Algernon*, p. 30.

40. Keyes, *Flowers for Algernon*, p. 35.

41. Keyes, *Flowers for Algernon*, p. 41.

42. Keyes, *Flowers for Algernon*, pp. 48–49.

43. Keyes, *Flowers for Algernon*, p. 50.

44. Keyes, *Flowers for Algernon*, p. 54.

45. Keyes, *Flowers for Algernon*, p. 75.

46. Keyes, *Flowers for Algernon*, p. 209.

47. Keyes, *Flowers for Algernon*, p. 216.

Chapter 4: The Characters

48. Keyes, *Flowers for Algernon*, p. 161.

49. Keyes, *Flowers for Algernon*, p. 75.

50. Keyes, *Flowers for Algernon*, p. 214.

51. Keyes, *Flowers for Algernon*, p. 72.

52. Keyes, *Flowers for Algernon*, p. 131.

53. Keyes, *Flowers for Algernon*, p. 186.

54. Keyes, *Flowers for Algernon*, p. 54.

55. Keyes, *Flowers for Algernon*, p. 132.

56. Keyes, *Flowers for Algernon*, p. 112.

57. Keyes, *Flowers for Algernon*, p. 63.

58. Keyes, *Flowers for Algernon*, p. 19.

Chapter 5: Themes of *Flowers for Algernon*

59. Keyes, *Flowers for Algernon*, p. 9.

60. Keyes, *Flowers for Algernon*, p. 11.

61. Keyes, *Flowers for Algernon*, p. 24.

62. Keyes, *Flowers for Algernon*, p. 22.

63. Keyes, *Flowers for Algernon*, p. 74.

64. Keyes, *Flowers for Algernon*, p. 55.

65. Keyes, *Flowers for Algernon*, p. 107.

66. *Times Literary Supplement* (London), "Making Up a Mind," July 21, 1966, p. 629.

67. Keyes, *Flowers for Algernon*, p. 71.

68. Keyes, *Flowers for Algernon*, p. 141.

69. Keyes, *Flowers for Algernon*, p. 88.

70. Keyes, *Flowers for Algernon*, p. 60.

71. Eliot Fremont-Smith, "The Message and the Maze," *New York Times*, March 7, 1966, p. 25.

72. Ronald Willis, "Flowers for Algernon," *books and bookmen*, September 1966, p. 34.

73. Keyes, *Flowers for Algernon*, p. 139.

74. Keyes, *Flowers for Algernon*, p. 138.

75. Keyes, *Flowers for Algernon*, pp. 172–73.

76. Keyes, *Algernon, Charlie and I*, p. 161.

77. Keyes, *Flowers for Algernon*, p. 12.

78. Keyes, *Flowers for Algernon*, p. 75.

79. Keyes, *Flowers for Algernon*, p. 112.

80. Keyes, *Flowers for Algernon*, p. 172.

81. Nicholls, *The Science Fiction Encyclopedia*, p. 330.

82. Keyes, *Flowers for Algernon*, p. 167.

83. Keyes, *Flowers for Algernon*, p. 179.

For Further Exploration

1. In the afterword to his autobiography, Daniel Keyes says that researchers think it will be possible to increase human intelligence with genetic engineering within thirty years. Imagine you are a scientist who has been given the novel *Flowers for Algernon* as an example of how such an experiment might turn out. Develop a policy statement on the ethical use of a procedure to increase human intelligence. Identify benefits and discuss ways to handle potential problems. Who would qualify for the procedures? Why? How would you make sure the mentally challenged person understands enough to agree to the procedure? Use examples from the novel to illustrate your points. *See also:* Daniel Keyes, *Algernon, Charlie and I: A Writer's Journey*. Boca Raton, FL: Challenge Press, 1999.

2. In a *Locus* magazine interview, Daniel Keyes says that he was determined to write *Flowers for Algernon* as a tragedy, even though several publishers thought the book should end happily. In this article, Keyes says that, based on what he learned in college about the ideas of the Greek philosopher Aristotle, "you cannot have a tragedy with someone who is low-born, you can only have a tragedy of the aristocracy, the elite, kings, because they have a *fall*." To achieve this, Keyes decided to "take the lowest of the low and raise him to the heights." Did Keyes succeed in making *Flowers for Algernon* a tragedy under that definition? If the book had ended happily, would it express the same themes? *See also: Locus*, "Daniel Keyes: 40 Years of Algernon," June 1997, p. 5.

3. Rewrite the first progress report of the novel in the third person point of view. Does the scene have the same emotional impact? If not, why? Explain how the technique of the first-person report contributes to or detracts from the reader's understanding of Charlie's character. *See also:* Thomas L. Wymer, Alice Calderonello, Lowell P. Leland, Sara Jayne Steen, and R. Michael Evers, eds., *Intersections: The Elements of Fiction in Science Fiction*. Bowling Green, OH: Popular Press, 1978, pp. 57–59.

4. After Charlie visits the Warren Home he says, "The feeling was of living death—or worse, of never having been fully alive and knowing." What is Charlie saying about his own situation? Does he feel the same at the very end of the book? Use events and

Charlie's thoughts to illustrate your answer. *See also: Times Literary Supplement* (London), "Making Up a Mind," July 21, 1966, p. 629.

5. Mr. Donner says to Charlie when he is about to fire him, "I treated you like my own son who gave up his life for his country." In what ways does Mr. Donner feel he has treated Charlie like a son? Does Charlie agree with Mr. Donner's characterization of their relationship? Do you? How does Mr. Donner's behavior compare with that of Matt Gordon, Charlie's real father? *See also:* Eliot Fremont-Smith, "The Message and the Maze," *New York Times,* March 7, 1966, p. 25.

6. Human behavior is sometimes at its worst when it is justified by the defense of "going along with the crowd." Describe instances from the novel when people do not act kindly toward Charlie, but do so because they are joining in with others. Do any characters think for themselves in defending or helping Charlie? Who? Whose behavior do you think is better and why? *See also:* Robert Scholes, *Structural Fabulation: An Essay on Fiction of the Future.* Notre Dame, IN: University of Notre Dame Press, 1975, pp. 56–57.

7. The sibling relationship between Charlie and Norma creates problems for both of them. Select examples of how the behavior of each bothers or hurts the other. Whom do you sympathize with? Why? What does Norma's reaction to the smart Charlie tell us about her childhood? *See also:* Eliot Fremont-Smith, "The Message and the Maze," *New York Times,* March 7, 1966, p. 25.

8. Keyes chose to make Algernon's progress and decline an important part of the book. How do Algernon's experiences help the reader understand Charlie's problems, feelings, and experiences? Why does Charlie let Algernon out of the cage at the scientific convention? Illustrate your answer with examples from the novel. *See also:* Peter Nicholls, ed., *The Science Fiction Encyclopedia.* Garden City, NY: Doubleday, 1979, p. 330.

9. Critic B. A. Young says of Charlie, "[H]e finds he was happier when stupid; what's more, he realizes from watching Algernon that the increased intelligence doesn't last. In the final pages he is back at subnormality and happy again." Do you agree with the critic's interpretation of Charlie's state of happiness? During what parts of the book does Charlie seem happy? Explain. What does

the last progress report show about Charlie's level of happiness? *See also:* B. A. Young, "First Novels," *Punch*, July 20, 1966, p. 125.

10. One sign of Charlie's increasing intelligence is that he recognizes moral dilemmas and takes the responsibility to deal with his feelings. Discuss three instances where Charlie has to judge whether his behavior or that of others is right or wrong. Do you agree with his assessment? Do you agree with how he then acts? *See also:* John J. Pierce, *Great Themes of Science Fiction: A Study of Imagination and Evolution.* New York: Greenwood Press, 1987, p. 27.

Appendix of Criticism

Charlie, the Character, "Finds" Daniel Keyes

I passed the New York Board of Education exam for an English teacher's license in June of 1957. With my higher salary as a regular teacher, [my wife] Aurea and I were able to rent a one-bedroom house in Seagate, a gated community at the western tip of Coney Island. I loved strolling the beach, smelling the salt air, looking out at the ocean and recalling my seafaring days. I set up my typewriter and desk in a corner of the bedroom, confident I'd be able to write in this place.

The following school term, the Chairman of the English department, impressed with my four published short stories, assigned me to teach two elective classes of creative writing. Each class was limited to twenty-five gifted students, all of whom loved reading and wanted to be writers. But many of them acted as if they deserved to have success handed to them because of their intelligence. When they groaned at the assignments and disdained revising their work, I told them, "There are those people who *want to write*, and others who *want to be writers*. For some geniuses, success comes without labor. For the rest of us, it's the love of writing that counts."

As if to compensate for these two "special classes," my other two classes were Special Modified English for low I.Q. students. For them, I expected to concentrate on spelling, sentence structure, and developing paragraphs. Class discussions focused on issues of the day that might interest them. The key to teaching the "special" students in "modified classes," I was told, is to motivate them with things relevant to their own lives.

I will never forget my first day of teaching one of the Special Modified English classes. I can still see the boy, in the rear of the room near the window. When the school bell rings at the end of the 50-minute-hour, students jump up and rush out—except that boy, who lumbers towards my desk. He wears a black parka, with the orange letter "J".

"Mr. Keyes . . . Can I ask you something?"

"Sure. You on the football team?"

"Yeah. Line-backer. Look, Mr. Keyes, this is a dummy class, isn't it?"

I'm taken aback. "What?"

"A dummy class . . . for stupid people . . ."

Not knowing how to react, I mumble, "No . . . not really . . . It's just *special* and *modified*. We go a little slower than some of the other—"

"I know this is a dummy class, and I wanted to ask you. *If I try hard and I get smart by the end of the term, will you put me in a regular class? I want to be smart.*"

"Sure," I say, not knowing if I really have the authority. "Let's see what happens."

When I get home that evening, I try to work on a story I've started, but the boy keeps intruding. His words: *"I want to be smart"* haunt me to this day. It never occurred to me that a developmentally challenged person—in those days they called it *retarded*—would be aware of his or her limitations and might want to be more intelligent.

I began to write about him [in short notes, but the story] was going nowhere. I put the notes away and forgot about them. . . .

Then, in the summer of 1958, H. L. Gold phoned and asked me to write a second story for *Galaxy* [magazine]. . . . It's amazing how quickly depression, frustration and demoralization can melt away when an editor asks a struggling writer for a story. I searched my files and notebooks.

There was that old, yellowed page from my first year at NYU with the line: *"I wonder what would happen if we could increase human intelligence artificially?"* I remembered my vision on the subway—*the wedge that intelligence has driven between me and my family. . . .*

I opened a more recent folder, turned several pages and saw the note:

A boy comes up to me in the Special Modified English class and says, "I want to be smart."

Stunned, I stared at those pages, side by side. A motivation collided with a *"What would happen if. . .?"*

Charlie Gordon—whoever you are, wherever you are—I hear you. I hear your voice calling out, *"Mr. Keyes, I want to be smart."*

Okay, Charlie Gordon, you want to be smart? I'll make you smart. Here I come, ready or not.

> Daniel Keyes, *Algernon, Charlie and I: A Writer's Journey.*
> Boca Raton, FL: Challenge Press, 1999.

A Modest Idea, Skillfully Executed

Algernon is a mouse and the flowers are for his grave, which explains the innervating title of this novel but does not convey Daniel Keyes's love of problems. "Flowers for Algernon," which had its origin as a much-anthologized short story (it was also a television drama and is now being made into a movie), is a technician's maze, a collection of nasty little challenges for a writer of fiction. That it works at all as a novel is proof of Mr. Keyes's deftness. And it is really quite a performance. He has taken the obvious, treated it in a most obvious fashion, and succeeded in creating a tale that is convincing, suspenseful and touching—all in modest degree, but it is enough. The obvious part is the message: We must respect life, respect one another, be kind to those less fortunate than ourselves. . . .

[Keyes's theme] is expounded in a tale consisting exclusively of Charlie Gordon's written journal, which progresses from primitive literacy to eloquence as it records his mental journey "into the light." Through it we learn that he has been chosen as the first human guinea pig for an experimental operation that can transform the severely retarded into intellectual giants. Perfected by Professor Nemur and Dr. Strauss, a psychiatrist, and backed by a foundation grant, the operation has been successfully performed on animals—one animal, anyway, Algernon the mouse, who now runs mazes like crazy. But how long the effect of the operation will last the doctors and psychologists don't know, nor do they know the emotional consequences of sudden intellectual advance in a person whose intellectual and emotional responses have been those of a 6-year-old.

Charlie's progress is rapid. In a matter of weeks, he is beating Algernon through the mazes, seeing pictures in the Rorschach tests, reading Dostoevsky, remembering past events—and learning that people are hypocritical, deceitful and cruel. He stumbles, of course, on love, and through some painful experiences and self-analysis he realizes that the old, retarded Charlie, maimed by his mother's desperate ambitions, is still inside him. He also realizes that the old Charlie, blind to the cruelty behind the laughter, had a modicum of happiness that is now lost. In fact, as he surpasses everyone in intelligence, his friends all turn on him in resentment: he is supposed to be the subject of an experiment, a prototype, a grateful product of scientific research; but he must, of course, be himself. What's worse, he discovers a terrible flaw in Professor Nemur's figures.

Now all of this is predictable, right down to the sad, inevitable end; it is a circular story with hardly a wiggle of variation. Predictable, too, are the problems of its first-person narration (credibility of misspellings, risks of repetition, pace of memory-recall, how to show Charlie convincingly a genius) and the patent incredibility of virtually everything that happens. On top of this are the dangers of sentimentality (those flowers for Algernon), pretentiousness (pseudopsychoanalytic delvings and sermonettes about the integrity of souls), too-easy humor (slapstick that can immediately undermine the delicate dignity of the book) and modesty (the circular business again; so small a conception that it may not seem to matter).

Mr. Keyes seems aware of all these problems and dangers; indeed, one senses a good deal of finger-exercising in the novel, and reads it with considerable technical fascination. Not every trap is avoided, but the skill shown here is awesome nonetheless. One might say that Mr. Keyes runs his maze at least as well as Algernon and Charlie run theirs, which is exciting in itself. And affecting, too—how otherwise explain the tears that come to one's eyes at the novel's end?

Eliot Fremont-Smith, "The Message and the Maze,"
New York Times, March 7, 1966.

An Effective Exploration of Human Character

Those who read [the short story "Flowers for Algernon"] when it first appeared in America in 1959 will welcome [the novel's] publication in [England], for it is a good example of that kind of science fiction which uses a persuasive hypothesis to explore emotional and moral issues. . . .

The narrator, Charlie Gordon, is a moron who allows himself to become the guinea pig for a team of neurosurgeons and psychologists who have developed a technique for increasing the intelligence of their subjects. The Algernon of the title is a mouse who has had the treatment first. The book consists of the reports written by Charlie as his intelligence changes. At first the super-Algernon is more intelligent, but slowly the man overtakes the mouse (spelling and syntax improving) and then he [overtakes] his mentors. All, however, is not gain. Once he thought that his workmates were laughing with him and he had good friends; he learns that they were laughing at him and he was [the] butt [of their jokes]. He is able to remember his early life, too, and gropes towards a painful understanding of the life of a family which contains a moron. His emergence from silly innocence means that his emotional maturity, though it lingers behind his developing I.Q., follows, struggling. His fits of irrational annoyance grow into a measured refusal to see himself as the creation of the scientists and an assertion that he was a man before they ever got to work on him.

By the time he is more intelligent than those who have given him his intellectual powers, he also knows what is wrong with their theories; as he watches Algernon degenerating into a normally stupid and abnormally baffled mouse, he knows that he will follow the same path.

In its ideas, especially in its speculations about the relationship between I.Q. and maturity, this is a far more intelligent book than the vast majority of "straight" [non–science fiction] novels. Moreover, the intelligence is displayed in a treatment of subject-matter which is bound to affect us as both important and moving. Charlie's hopeless knowledge that he is destined to end in a home for the feeble-minded, a moron who knows that he is a moron, is painful, and Mr. Keyes has the technical equipment to prevent us from shrugging off the pain.

Some of the subordinate characters are less successfully created and there are passages—notably those concerned with Charlie's need for sexual love—which encourage us to turn our attention more exclusively than the author intends to the ideas as distinct from the feelings of the people.

Times Literary Supplement (London),
"Making Up a Mind," July 21, 1966.

The Best Type of Science Fiction
Daniel Keyes had an exceptionally good idea for a work of fiction, and
the idea is what made it originally and still makes it a work of SF [sci-
ence fiction]. The idea is simply that an operation might be performed on a severely retarded adult male, which would enable his
mind not merely to catch up with those of his peers but actually to
surpass theirs. That is half of the idea. The other half, which com-
pletes and justifies this idea, is that the effects of the operation would
prove impermanent, so that the story involves our watching the protagonist grow into a genius unconsciously, and then consciously but
helplessly slip back toward a state of semi-literacy. When this mental
voyage has come full circle, the story is over.

For many people, I suspect, the first half of this idea constitutes the
domain of SF, a land of inconsequential wish-fulfillment in which the
natural laws that constitute the boundaries of human life are playfully
suspended. But the best writers of [SF] do not settle for mere imagi-
native play. Daniel Keyes completed the circuit of his idea, and the
beauty and power of the resulting story were acknowledged by his
readers at the eighteenth World Science Fiction Convention, where
he was awarded the Hugo [the top award]. It should be added that
Keyes's execution of his idea was fully adequate to the original conception. He undertook to present the story through a journal kept by
the protagonist himself, at the request of his doctor. Thus, we see the
growth of Charlie Gordon's mind through the evolution of his prose
style as well as in the events narrated. (Mr. Keyes, we might note,
happens to be an English teacher). Charlie acquires a competence in
grammar, an extensive lexicon, and a rich, vigorous syntax—and then
gradually loses all these, as his mental powers fade. He also becomes
an impatient, aggressive, arrogant, and unlovable man as his powers
increase, inspiring envy, jealousy, and even fear in others. But as he
loses his mental competence he regains the affection of those around
him—an affection grounded in pity, which is, . . . a form of contempt.

This tale . . . conveys to us the deprivation involved in mental retardation as no amount of reports or exhortations could possibly do it.

Robert Scholes,
Structural Fabulation: An Essay on Fiction of the Future.
Notre Dame, IN: University of Notre Dame Press, 1975.

A Successful Transformation from Short Story to Novel
There is hardly a reader inside the field [of science fiction] who is not
familiar with either the author's name or the [short] story title by
now. . . . The fact is, when I got the [novel], I didn't want to read it.
I remembered the [short] story too well, and I did not want to read a
padded-out, watered-down version. Unfortunately, the opening page

supported this sad expectation; and now that I have read it all—without putting it down, once I got started—I think the only real criticism I would make concerns some of the changes on the opening and closing pages.

The impact of the original [short] story rested primarily in the author's extraordinary—perhaps unique—success in conveying an identifiable-and-identifiable-*with* subjective portrait of a subnormal intelligence. Charlie Gordon was a moron, and he was also a man; the reader could accept him as a fellow-human, share his fears and hopes and desperate needs. . . . [In the novel, Keyes] has taken Charlie through intellectual, emotional, social, and sexual discoveries, and done it successfully. . . . I think it is less the technique (the first-person "Progress Report" method of the original story. . .), than the feeling that the projected shadow of a giant in the "simply" written diary is *real:* that somehow the author has managed to discern the actual shape of—if not the giant himself, then—the shadow, at least.

The novel is fully as remarkable an accomplishment as was the original story. I am sorry to have to include even my one small quibble—that some of the revisions in the very first and very last *progris riports* seemed to me to detract from, rather than add to, the original image of Charlie. Perhaps it is only that the paragraphs are longer; there is a bit more continuity of thought; Charlie seems to observe or understand more of *other* people's reactions. Or, perhaps, it is just that I do not want anything to change in my own almost personal vivid recollection of Charlie Gordon.

Judith Merril, review,
Magazine of Fantasy and Science Fiction, June 1966.

A Dynamic First-Person Narrator

Once an author has chosen his characters and setting and worked out his plot outline, he still has a decision to make which can radically affect the way we respond to the story: Who is going to tell it? Through whose eyes will we see the events unfold? How crucial this choice is can be suggested by imagining how different a hackneyed [worn-out] plot with stock hero, heroine and villain might be if it were told by the villain. The general term applied to this question of the position or positions from which we see the action and characters of a story is *point of view.* . . .

Because point of view concerns the question of what person is telling the story, it has become customary to divide the possible choices into broad categories according to the classifications provided by the personal pronouns. If the narrator refers to himself as "I" and tells a story of his personal experiences, the point of view is *first person;* if all characters are described by the narrator with pronouns like "he," "she," "it," "they," the point of view is *third person*. Within these broad categories, however, we can find an enormous variety of possibilities.

In the first person narrative the narrator is directly involved in plot by being a character in the story. . . . [I]nteresting effects can be produced when the [narrator-character] is dynamic, when, through his involvement in the action, he grows or otherwise changes so that the reader's understanding of the situation changes with him or her. This effect is accomplished to an extreme degree through the device of Charlie Gordon's "progress reports" in Daniel Keyes' "Flowers for Algernon." The reader senses the changes in Charlie as he grows from a mental retardate pathetically wishing he could be smart like everyone else—"They said Miss Kinnian told that I was her bestist pupil in the adult nite scool because I tried the hardist and I reely wantid to lern"—to a scientific genius appalled at the ignorance of the neurosurgeon who had altered his intelligence—"I was shocked to learn that the only ancient languages he could read were Latin, Greek, and Hebrew, and that he knows almost nothing of mathematics beyond the elementary levels of the calculus of variations." . . .

[A] first-person narrator's closeness to the action may be varied according to his position in time with respect to the action. We may, for example, be made aware of the fact that the narrator has completed the action of the story and is telling it to us or reporting it to the proper authority after the fact. He may thus hint at events to come or otherwise make us aware of himself as story teller, controlling suspense by withholding information he knows "now" but did not know "then." Or the author may try for a more natural sense of immediacy by the device of the journal. The narrator is keeping a journal or writing daily progress reports like Charlie Gordon or corresponding nightly to a friend. Thus at the time of writing he knows no more than he presents to us.

Thomas L. Wymer, Alice Calderonello, Lowell P. Leland, Sara Jayne Steen, and R. Michael Evers, eds.,
Intersections: The Elements of Fiction in Science Fiction.
Bowling Green, OH: Popular Press, 1978.

Chronology

1927
Keyes is born August 9 in Brooklyn, New York, to William and Betty Keyes.

1936
First use of prefrontal lobotomy, a type of brain surgery that attempted to improve behavior by disconnecting certain parts of the brain.

1937
Stanford-Binet IQ test revised.

1939
Wechsler-Bellevue adult IQ scale developed.

World War II begins in Europe.

1945
After completing one year of college at New York University, Keyes joins the U.S. Maritime Service as a senior assistant purser.

U.S. atomic bombs destroy Japanese cities of Hiroshima and Nagasaki, killing two hundred thousand and ending World War II.

1949
Wechsler Intelligence (IQ) Scale for Children published.

1950
Keyes graduates from Brooklyn College with a bachelor of arts in psychology.

First meeting of the group that would become the National Association for Retarded Children (today called Arc) is established to advocate for better treatment of the mentally handicapped.

1951
Keyes is named an associate fiction editor at Stadium Publishing, where he edits western, sports, and science fiction magazines and publishes his first stories (westerns) under an assumed name.

1952
Keyes marries Aurea Vazquez, a fashion stylist and photographer he met at a photography studio in New York City.

Keyes publishes his first magazine short stories in his own name: "Precedent" in *Marvel Science Fiction*, "Robot Unwanted" in *Other Worlds,* and "Something Borrowed" in *Fantastic Story.*

The United States detonates a hydrogen bomb five hundred times as powerful as the atomic bombs dropped on Japan.

Jonas Salk develops the polio vaccine.

Tranquilizers are marketed in the United States.

The first artificial heart valve is implanted in a human.

1953

Keyes becomes co-owner of a photography studio in New York City.

James Watson and Francis Crick describe the "double helix" model of DNA, opening the door to genetic mapping and engineering.

USSR detonates a hydrogen bomb.

1954

Keyes begins work as a high school English teacher in Brooklyn, New York.

The first successful kidney transplant is performed.

1955

Wechsler Adult Intelligence Scale published.

1958

Keyes's short story "The Trouble with Elmo" is published in *Galaxy* magazine.

1959

Keyes's short story "Flowers for Algernon" is published in *Magazine of Fantasy and Science Fiction*.

1960

Keyes receives the Science Fiction Achievement Award (the Hugo) from the World Science Fiction Society for "Flowers for Algernon."

Keyes's short story "Crazy Maro" is published in *Magazine of Fantasy and Science Fiction*.

Keyes's short story "The Quality of Mercy" is published in *IF* magazine.

Stanford-Binet IQ test revised.

1961

Keyes receives a master of arts degree from Brooklyn College in English and American literature.

Television airs an adaptation of "Flowers for Algernon."

President John F. Kennedy establishes the "President's Panel on Mental Retardation," which recommends the expansion of services to the mentally challenged.

1962
Keyes begins work as English instructor at Wayne State University in Detroit, Michigan.

Astronaut John Glenn is the first American to orbit the earth.

Cuban missile crisis erupts.

1963
Keyes's short story "A Jury of Its Peers" is published in *Worlds of Tomorrow.*

1966
Keyes's novel *Flowers for Algernon* is published and ties for a Nebula Award from the Science Fiction and Fantasy Writers of America.

Keyes begins work as a lecturer at Ohio University in Athens, Ohio.

1967
Keyes's story "Spellbinder" is published in *North American Review.*

1968
Charly (movie version of *Flowers for Algernon*) released.

Keyes's novel, *The Touch*, is published.

1972
Keyes is promoted to professor of English at Ohio University, Athens.

1973
Keyes is appointed to direct the creative writing center at Ohio University.

1975
The Education of All Handicapped Children Act is passed, requiring individualized public school programs for the mentally challenged.

1980
Keyes's novel *The Fifth Sally* is published.

1981
Keyes's nonfiction book *The Minds of Billy Milligan* is published, winning a special award from the Mystery Writers of America.

1986
Keyes's nonfiction book *Unveiling Claudia: A True Story of a Serial Murder* is published.

1988
Keyes is awarded the Brooklyn College "Distinguished Alumnus Medal of Honor."

1993
Daniel Keyes Collected Stories is published in Japan.

1994
The Milligan Wars, the sequel to *The Minds of Billy Milligan*, is published in Japan.

Daniel Keyes Reader is published in Japan.

1995
Harcourt Brace Modern Classics edition of *Flowers for Algernon* is published.

1998
Keyes's *Until Death Do Us Part: The Sleeping Princess* is published in Japan.

2000
Keyes's autobiography *Algernon, Charlie and I: A Writer's Journey* is released.

A new television adaptation of *Flowers for Algernon* airs on February 14, CBS TV, starring Matthew Modine as Charlie.

Ohio University honors Keyes as "Professor Emeritus."

Science Fiction Writers of America honors Keyes as "Author Emeritus."

Works Consulted

Major Editions of *Flowers for Algernon*
New York: Harcourt, Brace and World, 1966.
London: Cassell, 1966.
New York: Bantam Books, 1967.
New York: Bantam Books, 1975.
New York: Harcourt Brace Modern Classics edition, 1995.
Audiotape, read by Daniel Keyes. Fremont, CA: Parrot Audio Books Productions, 1995. Abridged.
Audiotape, read by Jeff Woodman. New York: Recorded Books Productions, 1998. Unabridged.

Major Adaptations
The Two Worlds of Charlie Gordon, TV movie, 1961.
Charly, movie, 1968.
"Flowers for Algernon," TV movie, 2000.

Also by Daniel Keyes
Daniel Keyes, *The Fifth Sally.* Boston: Houghton Mifflin, 1980. The fictional story of a woman with multiple personalities.

———,"Flowers for Algernon," *Magazine of Fantasy and Science Fiction*, April 1959. The original short story. Also anthologized in *Ten Top Stories.* New York: Bantam Books, 1975.

———,*The Minds of Billy Milligan.* New York: Bantam Books, 1999. A nonfiction account of a man with twenty-four personalities who was acquitted of serious crimes by reason of insanity.

———,*The Touch.* New York: Harcourt, Brace and World, 1968. The fictional story of a pregnant woman and her husband who have been exposed to radiation.

———,*Unveiling Claudia.* New York: Bantam Books, 1986. A true-crime account of a woman who confessed to multiple murders.

Biographical Information
Anne Commire, ed., "Daniel Keyes," in *Something About the Author.* Vol. 37. Detroit, MI: Gale Research, 1985. A biographical sketch that includes the important landmarks in Keyes's personal life and career.

Daniel Keyes, *Algernon, Charlie and I: A Writer's Journey*. Boca Raton, FL: Challenge Press, 1999. An autobiography that explains why and how Keyes wrote his most famous novel. Includes the full text of the 1959 short story, "Flowers for Algernon."

Daniel Keyes (http://in.flite.net/~dkeyes). Includes summaries of Keyes's books, a brief biography, and answers frequently asked questions about *Flowers for Algernon*. Includes updated information on adaptations of the novel.

Locus, "Daniel Keyes: 40 Years of Algernon," June 1997. A capsule version of Keyes's autobiography. Also includes a discussion of Keyes's other works and his success outside the United States. Excerpt available online at www.locusmag.com/1997/issues/06/Keyes.html.

Peter Nicholls, ed., *The Science Fiction Encyclopedia*. Garden City, NY: Doubleday, 1979. Includes a short biographical sketch of Keyes, and articles on how *Flowers for Algernon* fits into the science fiction genre.

Daniel Keyes is represented by the William Morris agency in New York. For more information about the author, consult the following:

Contemporary Authors (Vol. 10).

Contemporary Authors (Vol. 81) contains chapters 1–8 of the new work, *Algernon, Charlie, and I: A Writer's Journey*, as an autobiographical essay.

Something About the Author (Vol. 37).

Contemporary Literary Criticism (Vol. 80).

"In Search of the Novel," a ten-hour series, produced by the Corporation for Public Broadcasting, includes interviews with Daniel Keyes.

Keyes's Papers and manuscripts are held in "The Daniel Keyes Collection," Alden Library, Ohio University, Athens, Ohio.

Historical and Scientific Background

American Psychoanalytic Association (http://apsa.org/index.htm). Official website of a professional organization of psychoanalysts. Includes explanations and history, links to additional information. Provides lists of practicing psychoanalysts who are members of the association.

The Arc of the United States (http://thearc.org). The official website of the national organization on mental retardation. Summarizes the organization's support and advocacy activities. Includes history of, and descriptions of services for, the mentally retarded.

Francis Leone, *Genetics: The Mystery and the Promise*. Blue Ridge Summit, PA: TAB Books, 1992. A challenging book for science-oriented readers that tells the history and science behind modern genetics. Includes a discussion about the consequences and ethics of genetic engineering.

Romayne Smith, ed., *Children with Mental Retardation: A Parents' Guide*. Rockville, MD: Woodbine House, 1993. Thoughtful essays by experts on the history, diagnosis, and treatment of mental retardation. Includes advice about family and community life and legal rights. Lists resources.

Martin Walker, *The Cold War: A History*. New York: Henry Holt, 1993. Comprehensive and readable study of the cold war.

Science Fiction Criticism

John J. Pierce, *Great Themes of Science Fiction: A Study of Imagination and Evolution*. New York: Greenwood Press, 1987. Discusses early examples of superman or intelligence science fiction.

Robert Scholes, *Structural Fabulation: An Essay on Fiction of the Future*. Notre Dame, IN: University of Notre Dame Press, 1975. Discusses Keyes's use of a science fiction event to explore significant themes.

Thomas L. Wymer, Alice Calderonello, Lowell P. Leland, Sara Jayne Steen, and R. Michael Evers, eds., *Intersections: The Elements of Fiction in Science Fiction*. Bowling Green, OH: Popular Press, 1978. Discusses *Flowers for Algernon* as an example of a science fiction novel written in the first person.

Reviews

Eliot Fremont-Smith, "The Message and the Maze," *New York Times*, March 7, 1966. The author says that Keyes took a modest idea and presented it with great technical skill.

Marilyn Krzywkowski, "Flowers for Algernon," English Journal, May 1966. A college student reviewer praises Keyes for his skill in characterizing Charlie.

Judith Merril, "Flowers for Algernon," *Magazine of Fantasy and Science Fiction*, June 1966. The author says that the transformation from short story to novel was mostly successful.

Times Literary Supplement (London), "Making Up a Mind," July 21, 1966. The author believes the novel is a fine example of the use of science fiction to explore important themes.

Ronald Willis, "Flowers for Algernon," *books and bookmen*, September 1966. The author says that the novel makes readers consider how they could have been like Charlie.

B. A. Young, "First Novels," *Punch*, July 20, 1966. The author found the novel unsubtle but interesting.

Index

Picture Credits

About the Author

Patrice Cassedy received an undergraduate degree in English from the University of Michigan, where she published her first article and held her first post as a magazine editor. After graduating from Rutgers law school in Camden, New Jersey, she pursued dual careers as a corporate attorney and an author. She has also worked as nonfiction editor for a literary magazine based in San Diego.

She is temporarily living in the Washington, D.C., area with her husband and her middle-school-age daughteer, Eva. The Cassedys plan to return to Southern California, where son Michael attends college.

Cassedy enjoys sharing her children's interests, including jazz music, creative writing, and basketball. In her free time, she likes traveling, walking, and surfing the Net. She continues to do specia legal projects while pursuing her writing career.